AF428701

THE SCIENCE-BACKED ANTI-INFLAMMATORY DIET FOR BEGINNERS

A **Hassle-Free Guide and Simple Meal Plan** to Enhance Immunity, Optimize Gut Health, and Reduce Chronic Pain at Any Age

YASMINE ELAMIR, MD

WILLIAM GRIST, MD

TABLE OF CONTENTS

INTRODUCTION

Chronic inflammation is considered one of the greatest risks to humans, as it is the highest cause of death throughout the world. A total of 60% of people suffer from some sort of chronic inflammatory disease, such as diabetes, obesity, heart disease, and many more (Pahwa et al., 2023). Many of these inflammatory diseases are caused by a poor diet, which can cause not only weight concerns but can also trigger inflammatory responses that can lead to chronic inflammation or even autoimmune diseases. However, it's always easy to say that one should eat healthily and get enough exercise, but what is a healthy diet and enough exercise? What works for one person may not work for another. There seems to be a lack of necessary information needed by those who are concerned about inflammatory diseases.

The best way to fight inflammation—and all the diseases associated with it—is to look at your diet. Nutrition is vital. What you eat is more than the fuel your body needs to do daily tasks; it affects everything from your DNA to your health. Good fuel results in good health, while poor fuel will result in poor health. Good nutrition helps to maintain a healthy weight, lowers the risk of developing many diseases, and lowers high blood pressure and cholesterol while boosting energy levels, the immune system, and your well-being and lowering the recovery time from illnesses and injuries.

A diet should be filled with macronutrients (protein, carbs, and good fats), micronutrients (minerals and vitamins), as well as fiber and plenty of water. However, not all diets contain food that will fuel you. Fast food may be convenient, with lives being as rushed as they are, but they are slowly shortening life spans. Food high in unhealthy fats, salt, and sugar may let you feel good, but they're full of things that can trigger inflammation. Not only that, but these convenient foods are low in fiber, meaning your gut microbiome isn't receiving the food it needs to thrive and help with improving your health. By consuming a poor diet, your cells won't have the necessary energy to carry out their functions, leading to the repair and maintenance falling behind. This results in exhaustion and a struggle to find the energy to do what you want, much less what you have to.

However, trying to create a diet to combat inflammation is tiresome and confusing because of the conflicting information flooding the internet—especially when people are trying to sell "miracle cures." Because of all this conflicting information, it's difficult to find the necessary anti-inflammatory recipes required for them to still be considered healthy and tasty. Not to mention, some recipes are complicated or time-consuming.

Yet it isn't just about recipes. Having one good meal, now and again, isn't going to fix any inflammatory problems, it requires dedication and a meal plan to be in place before you start. However, due to the uniqueness of people, it can be difficult to find a meal plan that considers all your needs. If you can't find a meal plan that works for you, you won't stick to the diet, and you'll fall back on old habits—including poor diet.

You may have already tried a change in diet and found that it did nothing for you, making you believe that a dietary change can't fix the problems you're experiencing. Not to mention that verified diets, medical guidance, and expertise are often behind a paywall. As a result, your research into managing your inflammatory diseases may lead you to use unverified and sometimes poor information. Not only will this worsen what symptoms you may already be suffering, but it can crush your spirit in finding a way to help you live a better life!

So instead of diving into a myriad of information, not knowing whether it's true or not, explore this book, which is conveniently divided into three parts, making it easier to navigate.

Within Part 1, you'll learn about what inflammation is and how an anti-inflammatory diet will help you fight against the increasing risk of chronic inflammation and the diseases associated with it.

In Part 2, you'll be invited to try delectable breakfasts, boosting lunches, appetizing snacks, and even a few surprises for the holiday season, so you don't have to feel left out. The recipes are so good that you can share them with everyone without anyone being the wiser.

Then, in Part 3, you'll learn how to keep a health journal, so you can see your progress while on the 21-day meal plan to help you overcome any inflammation you may be suffering.

 The Science-Backed Anti-Inflammatory Diet for Beginners

You may be thinking that this book is like so many others. False promises and hopes are dashed when all you want is to be free of pain. It's vital to remember that this book is only providing you with the necessary information to make the best choice for your health. When it comes to a new diet, consistency is key. Knowing this, together with all the guiding information within this book, you'll find that an anti-inflammatory diet will help you not only lose weight (especially when lowering your intake of excess calories), but there will be an improvement in inflammation symptoms, pain, heart health, fasting glucose, and body condition.

With this book, you'll learn to identify and eliminate foods that cause inflammation from your diet, allowing your body to heal naturally without excess medication. By ensuring that your diet is filled with at least 80% anti-inflammatory foods, you'll be improving your life and thrive.

All you need to do is make a few smart changes to bring about a better life. What do you have to lose? The weight? The painful and possibly deadly inflammatory disease? That all sounds like a win-win situation.

As you explore the various chapters of this book, you'll learn about

- the different types of inflammation and how it can be combated

- the gut's influence on inflammation

- inflammation's hand in weight, menopause, and heart issues

- how to determine your individual needs for an anti-inflammatory diet and how to address them

- how to identify and cut out foods that trigger inflammation

- how to cook a variety of healthy, tasty, and filling meals and snacks suited to your individual needs

- how to stick to a meal plan

- how to keep a health journal

- and so much more

While it can be difficult to trust any old book—due to false information everywhere—this one is different. All the information presented in this book is from two married physicians who practice what they preach! All we want to do is show you that there is a holistic way to improve inflammatory disease by making a healthy change in your lifestyle and diet, all changes we have brought into our own lives and for the better.

Change is difficult without guidance, so take this book with you on your journey to fighting back against inflammation and the risks associated with it. With all the knowledge that we have spent years gathering and implementing, we will be the guidance you need to help you take the necessary positive steps to improve your life through small changes. All you need to do now is to turn to the next chapter to dive into a world where you take charge and fight back against unnecessary inflammation.

PART 1

A GLIMPSE INTO THE ANTI-INFLAMMATORY DIET

In this section, we'll look at what inflammation is, how it affects your life, and how it can be combated with diet and determine what foods are likely to trigger inflammation.

CHAPTER 1

THE SCIENCE BEHIND

A total of 50% of all deaths worldwide are caused by diseases stemming from chronic inflammation (Furman et al., 2019). This includes ischemic heart disease, autoimmune diseases, type 2 diabetes, and so many more. None of these diseases just happen, it takes time to develop, and there are warning signs. The increased risk of developing these chronic diseases starts early, carrying into adulthood, contributing to the increased risk of early death. However, what is inflammation, and how does it influence your body and health?

INFLAMMATION AND ITS EFFECTS ON THE BODY

Inflammation isn't inherently bad; it serves a function as the body's first line of defense. It lets the body know that something is wrong and that it should take steps to address the problem.

When a foreign invader (bacteria, viruses, etc.) or an injury occurs, the immune system kicks in with its first responders. This includes inflammatory cells and cytokines, which stimulate the body to make more inflammatory cells. The inflammatory cells have many functions. Some will fight against invaders, while others will start the healing process. There are two types of inflammation, acute and chronic.

Acute inflammation	Chronic inflammation
Usually occurs when there is a sudden injury, and the body responds quickly.	The inflammation continues for an extended period and may not be noticed for some time.
Once the healing occurs, the inflammation dies back.	Inflammation continues for a long time, in some cases for years.
Acute inflammation's common symptoms that last a few days include swelling, localized heat, redness, and a temporary decrease in functionality in an affected limb.	Signs of chronic inflammation are subtle but will progressively worsen as time goes by.
Acute inflammation is usually caused by injury, infection, or exposure to a foreign substance (dust).	Common symptoms may mimic flu-like symptoms (fever, muscle stiffness, chills, etc.). There may even be fatigue, skin rashes, mouth sores, joint pain and stiffness, and chest or abdomen pain later on.

While acute inflammation is less serious than chronic inflammation, if ignored long enough, it can become chronic—especially if a wound festers without treatment. Over time, chronic inflammation will spread, resulting in diseases such as type 2 diabetes, certain cancers, Alzheimer's disease, rheumatoid arthritis, and more, as different areas of the body become affected.

Chronic inflammation can also be caused by the immune system overreacting to a foreign body and, in turn, will continue to keep inflammation in place, even after the problem has been dealt with. In other cases, a foreign substance is similar to something completely harmless, causing the harmless thing to be attacked as if it were a danger to the body. This can result in allergies and asthma. In severe cases, the body starts to attack itself, causing autoimmune diseases.

HOW AN ANTI-INFLAMMATORY DIET HELPS

Ideally, you want to stop your body from turning against you, but even if it has already, there are ways to fight back. The best way to do this isn't always medication but by looking at what you're consuming.

Convenient, prepackaged fast foods may save you time, but they are slowly causing your body to turn against itself. Processed foods are known to be high in added sugars, fried fats, and too much salt, all causes of increased free radicals that cause inflammation. However, it isn't just junk food that is contributing to the rise of inflammation. It's the lack of anti-inflammatory foods.

As the body metabolizes the food we eat, it produces free radicals that can go on to cause many problems from premature aging to increasing inflammatory responses. Consuming a diet high in foods that contain antioxidants (fruits, vegetables, and whole grains) allows the body to combat the damage caused by free radicals. The best way to get antioxidants is to eat a diet containing a wide range of whole (unrefined) foods. There are various antioxidants, and each will help improve your life. Here's a list of some foods that help lower inflammation.

Drinks	Preferably water (water infusions with herbs, spices, fruits, and vegetables), limited fruit juice (ideally watered down), tea (green), and limited coffee
Fatty fish	Salmon, tuna, herring, anchovies, sardines, and mackerel
Fruits	Cherries, berries (blackberries and blueberries), strawberries, olives, avocados, grapefruit, bananas (high in sugar but have good fiber), apples, and grapes—the brighter the fruit, the better
Grains	Whole grains, such as whole wheat, or gluten-free options, such as oatmeal, amaranth, or millet if gluten-sensitive

Healthy fats	Extra virgin olive oil, also known as EVOO (regular olive oil is fine too), and avocado oil
Herbs and spices	Turmeric, ginger, fenugreek, and cinnamon (play around with different spices and herbs to help you use less sugar and salt in your cooking)
Legumes	Beans, peas, lentils, tofu, seitan, and chickpeas
Nuts and seeds	Almonds, walnuts, chia seeds, pumpkin seeds, and flaxseeds (you can also enjoy different seeds and nut butter)
Miscellaneous	Pro- and prebiotics, dark chocolate (at least 70% cocoa), and red wine (limited), as it contains healthy polyphenols
Vegetables	Dark green vegetables (kale, broccoli, spinach, etc.), cauliflower, Brussels sprouts, and bell peppers (all the colors)

Some of the best anti-inflammatory diets include the Mediterranean, the Dietary Approaches to Stop Hypertension (DASH), and the hybrid of the two, the Mediterranean–DASH Intervention for Neurodegenerative Delay (MIND). The Mediterranean diet has long been heralded as the healthiest diet due to its known anti-inflammatory foods high in fiber, healthy fats, and lean proteins, with limited consumption of red meat and the avoidance of all processed goods. The DASH diet helps lower inflammatory markers while lowering high blood pressure and the risk of gout with less uric acid in the food consumed. While these diets will help you on your journey to lowering chronic inflammation, there is no need to stick to one of the three. As long as you're consuming a variety of nutrient-dense foods, with a wide range of antioxidants, and healthy fats with lean protein, you'll make a difference.

However, even if something looks healthy, it doesn't necessarily mean it is. While whole grains are required in a healthy diet, if you're gluten-sensitive or have a gluten allergy, it will increase inflammation. You will need to explore gluten-free grains to prevent a reaction. Similarly, people who are lactose intolerant will need to avoid dairy products and find alternatives to getting the necessary calcium and vitamin D to keep their bones healthy.

Other foods that may cause problems are cruciferous vegetables (from the Brassica family, including broccoli, cauliflower, etc.) and those from the nightshade family (tomato, eggplant, potato, and sweet and hot peppers).

IMMUNITY AND GUT HEALTH CONNECTION

Your gut and digestion begins at your mouth and ends at the anus. Many organs form part of your gut that aid in the digestion and absorption of food. However, it isn't just your body that plays a vital role. Within you, there are millions of microorganisms (viruses, bacteria, yeasts, and more) that make up the gut microbiome that helps with many functions to keep you in good health. The gut microbiome does so much work, it's considered by many as another organ that lives symbiotically with us.

The gut plays an important role in your immunity as up to 70% of it is housed within the intestinal lining where the gut-associated lymphoid tissue (GALT) is hosted (Carver-Carter, 2022). This tissue houses the lymphoid immune cells and coordinates the inflammatory responses within the gut while allowing harmless microbes to pass unharmed.

This immunity can be influenced by the gut microbes in several ways. The first is that gut microbes can digest indigestible fibers and resistant starches through fermentation. This creates short-chain fatty acids, which assist in immune homeostasis, strengthen the gut wall, lower inflammation, and help regular T-cells (the cells responsible for calming the immune system after it's activated).

The diversity and balance of the gut microbes also play a vital role in your health, as they can stimulate or prevent inflammation depending on the diversity and balance. When the gut microbes are balanced (more good microbes than pathogenic), the body works as it should, allowing the immune system to function correctly. A correctly functioning immune system maintains harmony within the body, leading to immune homeostasis, resulting in the immune system fighting problems the way it should. A high

   The Science-Backed Anti-Inflammatory Diet for Beginners

diversity aids in the production of interleukin-10, an anti-inflammatory cytokine that helps to lower inflammation.

However, if something disturbs the harmony and diversity of the gut microbes, it can lead to dysbiosis, where the pathogenic microbes have a stronger foothold, leading to illness. Dysbiosis and low diversity are often associated with chronic inflammation, resulting in increased risks of developing gut issues such as ulcerative colitis, inflammatory bowel disease (IBD), and Crohn's disease. This disruption could also lead to disrupted immune homeostasis, causing the immune system to overreact to the smallest issue, leading to eczema, allergies, and asthma.

As long as the gut is balanced and has a high diversity of good microbes, it encourages the healthy immune cells in the GALT, which then become better at their job of recognizing true pathogenic invaders from harmless microbes. However, that's not to say that pathogenic invaders can't still harm you. Some release toxic chemicals, which are pro-inflammatory, upon their death. These chemicals activate cytokines and T-helper cells, both of which cause an immune response and increased inflammation.

Another negative of dysbiosis is that it can cause an increase in permeability in the intestinal lining. A healthy intestinal lining will allow nutrients to travel through specific cells into the blood, where they are then taken to where they are required. However, during dysbiosis, the permeability increases, allowing undigested food and other foreign items to leave the intestines and float into the blood, causing an immune response that could affect the entire body. This is known as leaky gut syndrome, and while not a recognized medical diagnosis, it's considered one of the reasons for the occurrence of widespread inflammation, such as systemic lupus erythematosus.

There's a lot of current research exploring the link between gut microbes and their influence on the immune system and their effect on inflammatory diseases, ranging from how dysbiosis causes different diseases to how the gut microbiome can be used to improve health physically, mentally, and even emotionally.

WEIGHT LOSS AND CARDIOVASCULAR BENEFITS

Cardiovascular disease causes a third of deaths in America (Li et al., 2020). Heart disease can be caused by many different factors such as genetics, viruses, and poor diet. One of the main causes of heart disease is atherosclerosis, caused by plaque buildup due to high cholesterol. However, this can be worsened when the body is experiencing increased inflammation.

What you eat will affect your heart. Diets high in red and processed meat, refined grains, added sugars, fried foods, and excess salt promote inflammation, which can lead to increased risks of heart attacks and other coronary diseases. In a study that spanned 32 years, with over 290,000 participants, it was found that people who ate pro-inflammatory foods suffered a 38% increased risk of developing heart diseases compared to those who ate healthier diets (Li et al., 2020). Those who ate more whole grains, fruits, vegetables, healthy fats, and lean protein had lower incidences of heart problems during the course of the study.

The increased inflammation caused by the pro-inflammatory foods will eventually lead to chronic inflammation, resulting in increased inflammatory markers, increasing the risk of not only heart issues but also strokes. Eating an anti-inflammatory diet helps to lower these biomarkers such as interleukin-6, C-reactive protein, cytokines, and others, helping to lower the inflammation and the risk of heart disease. However, it's important to remember that this isn't a quick fix. It takes time to reach a level of inflammation that negatively affects your health, so it will take time for the diet to take effect, but it will help from the first day you decide to make the change.

It's not only your heart that can benefit from an anti-inflammatory diet, but your weight will also be affected. The anti-inflammatory diet encourages a variety of whole foods while restricting junk food that leads to inflammation. As you are no longer eating or drinking foods that are high in empty calories in favor of nutrient-dense meals, you may find that you will start to lose weight. However, it isn't the goal of an anti-inflammatory diet to assist in weight loss; it's just a happy coincidence.

In the study conducted by Kenđel Jovanović et al. (2020), obese participants were put on an anti-inflammatory diet for six months, resulting in them losing 7% of their total body weight as well as a decrease in their inflammation. However, this study also restricted their calorie intake and was a contributing factor to the weight loss.

ANTI-INFLAMMATORY DIET AND MENOPAUSE

An anti-inflammatory diet may even help you with menopause side effects. Menopause is something all women will experience as they age. Premenopause starts at 45–55, and menopause occurs 12 months after a woman experiences their last menstrual cycle. The ovaries start to secrete lower levels of the hormones estrogen and progesterone, resulting in side effects such as hot flashes, night sweats, increased weight, joint pain, mood changes, and poor sleep, just to name a few. Another terrible side effect is that the body's fat cells will start producing estrogen to make up for the lack of the hormone, resulting in added inches around the middle that are difficult to lose. This weight is often associated with the development of type 2 diabetes. Thankfully, a dietary change can assist with lowering the severity of the side effects of menopause.

The anti-inflammatory diet contains a variety of plant-based foods that are high in phytoestrogens. These plant chemicals, found in tofu, pumpkin seeds, and dried apricots, mimic the effects of estrogen but at a lower strength than the hormone. Phytoestrogens help to ease hot flashes in some women and will take 2–3 months after a dietary change to have an effect. However, after this time, the frequency of hot flashes is less, and they are more manageable.

It isn't only the phytoestrogens that play a crucial role, the minerals and vitamins also have a part to play. Osteoporosis is a disease prevalent in women undergoing menopause, causing the calcium to be leached from their bones, making them weaker and leading to more fractures. Estrogen has anti-inflammatory properties and helps protect joints, so as its concentration decreases, you may also experience more joint pain than normal and have low levels of chronic inflammation. Consuming any pro-inflammatory foods will aggravate the joints, making the pain worse. Consuming more seeds, nuts, whole grains, fruits, and vegetables gives you the necessary vitamins and minerals that promote bone health and strengthen them against fractures.

The addition of more fish to your diet will also benefit your bones and also give additional omega-3 fatty acids to help lower inflammation. Then there are spices such as turmeric and ginger that can improve your health. Turmeric helps your microbiome remain stable, as they're negatively affected by hormonal changes. As you age, you have fewer digestive enzymes to help boost your digestion and aid in moving food through your digestive tract. Due to this, ginger is a must, dried or fresh.

Menopause doesn't need to ruin your life. Changing your diet to incorporate more anti-inflammatory foods will help ease the symptoms of menopause, lowering the risk of osteoporosis, improving sleep quality, stabilizing blood sugar levels, lowering chronic inflammation, and improving gut health.

Consider your body's inflammation an internal fire. When you have it under control, everything is well, but when it is out of control, it causes destruction in your body, resulting in various inflammatory diseases. Your immune system is in charge of handling inflammation, but it can be influenced by external and internal forces, especially with changes to the gut microbiome. A balanced and highly diverse microbiome will ensure a healthy and stable immune system, but dysbiosis will lead to increased intestinal permeability, inflammatory biomarkers, and an immune system attacking indiscriminately.

The best way to keep your gut happy is to have a diet that helps lower inflammation while still providing all the nutrition you need. To do this, you need to understand how to cut out poor foods and foods that trigger inflammatory responses. In the next chapter, you'll learn practical and easy-to-understand guidelines on how to develop and use the anti-inflammatory diet.

CHAPTER 2

GETTING STARTED

Modern society is quick to run to a doctor if they feel something is wrong with them. They do this without considering that the problem may be caused by what they put into their body. While doctors and other medical professionals are required for many incidences, they can't change how you live your life; only you can do that. So before you book an appointment with your closest doctor's office, turn your eye to your kitchen to find the key to taking control of your life and fighting back against inflammation.

ASSESSING INDIVIDUAL NEEDS

Although most countries have general guidelines for diet and nutrition, this isn't adequate for everyone. No one is the same, and that is why all diets should be tailored to the needs of the person it's being given to. With a tailored diet, your unique needs are considered, therefore creating a diet that will work for you, as long as you're consistent with sticking to it.

Consider milk. It's high in calcium and when fortified contains vitamins A and D, helping to strengthen bones and teeth. All of these are required for a healthy diet. However, if you are lactose intolerant, milk will bring you nothing but misery with bloat, painful gas, diarrhea, and nausea.

DETERMINING YOUR DIETARY REQUIREMENTS

Tailored diets aim to provide the necessary nutrients and calorie requirements for your unique situation. It takes into consideration your age, genetics, medical history, life stage, and activity levels, and while it sounds complicated, it only needs a little research from you to determine what you need for a diet. Here are some handy steps to help you decide what you need:

1. Identify what you want from your diet.

   - Do you want to lose weight or lower chronic inflammation?

2. Consider your needs due to a life stage change.

   - When pregnant or breastfeeding, women need more iron and folic acid while lowering the amount of fish they eat due to excess mercury.

   - Anyone older than 50 should consider getting more B12 in their diet.

3. Assess current eating patterns.

   - Start a food journal and jot down everything you eat in as much detail as possible. Be honest with yourself, as this information will be necessary later.

   - Take note of how often you eat foods that are considered "bad" for you.

4. Take note of dietary constraints.

   - Some preferred diets may have nutritional shortcomings that will need to be rectified with supplements or by exploring alternative foods.

   - Diets such as veganism and the keto diet are known for lacking certain vitamins and minerals.

5. Know the general recommendations for your country's diet and build from it.

   - A standard 2,000-calorie diet should have at least 3 ounces of whole grains, 2 ½ cups of vegetables, 2 cups of fruit, up to 3 cuts of low-fat milk products, and 5–6 ounces of plant-based sources of protein or lean protein.

6. Determine your calorie needs.

    - Many factors play a role in calorie needs from age and gender to activity level.

    - Sedentary women 18–34 require 1,800–2,000 calories, while the same age group that is active will need 2,200–2,400.

    - Sedentary men 18–34 require 2,200–2,600 calories, while those who are active will need as much as 2,800–3,000.

7. Know your activity levels, as this will determine if you need to compensate with more food.

    - Ideally, 75 minutes of vigorous exercise or 150 minutes of moderate exercise a week, with 2–3 days of strength building, is what you need to stay healthy.

8. Learn how to understand nutritional labels and the difference between a portion and a serving size.

    - Portions are the size of the item eaten, while the serving is the standardized amount of that item that should be eaten.

    - A medium apple is one serving, while a large apple is more, despite it still being one portion.

    - Knowing what is on the nutritional labels allows you to make smarter choices about your food, and you can use the ingredient list to know exactly what's in your food.

9. Employ a food tracker to help you keep track of the nutritional information of what you're eating. Use this in conjunction with your food diary.

    - FatSecret, MyFitnessPal, and Lose It! are some available apps. Some features may require a monthly subscription.

    - The tracker allows you to record your diet and can be updated with each meal you consume. It may seem like a lot of work, but it'll be easier to identify problem foods in the long run.

- This requires you to be honest with what you're writing, or your eating behaviors won't change.

Once you've gone through all these instructions, you need to consider how your diet will slot into your lifestyle and schedule. Elaborate, albeit healthy, meals take time to make, and if your job keeps you on your feet all the time, a sit-down meal may not be for you. Thankfully, many different recipes allow an anti-inflammatory diet to be as conforming to your life as possible.

What meals you decide to prepare yourself will need to align with your daily routine, making it easier to work with. You will also need to consider variety while remaining consistent with your diet. Eating the same meals daily will result in boredom and nutrient deficiencies, both of which can break a diet before it begins. Lastly, don't forget to be flexible. While many food types can cause inflammation, many of those food types may be some of your favorites. Highly restrictive diets are just as bad as poor diets. Indulging once in a while on foods that fall outside the anti-inflammatory diet won't break the diet and allows you to feel better after having a small treat. However, be sure to only include treats that don't trigger immune responses that can cause inflammation.

UNDERSTANDING ALLERGIES, INTOLERANCES, AND SENSITIVITIES

The inner workings of your body are influenced by what you eat. Over time, the body can develop sensitivities, intolerances, and allergies around food, some of which can be caused by the body becoming very sensitive because of inflammation. While these phrases are sometimes used interchangeably, they aren't the same.

Food sensitivity	Food intolerance	Food allergy
This causes an immune response to a specific group of foods (gluten-containing) or one food type.	The body is lacking the necessary enzymes to break down a certain type of food, and there is no immune response.	This causes a severe immune response to a type of food with increased production of the antibody immunoglobulin E (IgE).
Symptoms include migraines, brain fog, and digestive issues, which are usually subtle and slow to appear.	Symptoms are normally limited to digestive discomfort and pain.	Symptoms include swollen tongue or airway, hives, and difficulty breathing or swallowing.
This is generally not life-threatening.	This is generally not life-threatening.	Reaction occurs quickly and can be life-threatening if left untreated.

Food allergies are quickly discovered in children and in some cases adults, later in life, and the culprit food is removed from the diet. However, food sensitivities are subtle, and they aren't always noticed at first, but because there is an immune response, it can become chronic over time. To avoid these sensitivities leading to a full-blown allergy, they need to be discovered and treated.

While there are home testing kits for food sensitivities, they aren't accurate enough to determine what food is causing the reaction or whether it is a sensitivity and not a typical response to eating food. Never use a home testing kit to diagnose yourself with a food sensitivity or allergy. With the possibility of a false positive, it can lead to anxiety and fear about eating specific foods for no reason. Many of the tests use the presence of immunoglobulin G (IgG) and immunoglobulin G4 (IgG4) to determine if there is a sensitivity or allergy, and this isn't accurate or reliable.

If you suspect there is a food that's causing problems, make a list of the foods and the symptoms you're experiencing. The list can then be taken to your doctor or an allergist, who can do the necessary test to determine if there is a sensitivity or allergy. The test can be done by looking at your blood or skin reactions. The specialist will look at the results of your test and your food journal to determine if you are experiencing allergies or sensitivities. This is the best way to determine which foods need to be cut from your diet, and they will also tell you which similar foods or food components are best avoided. Armed with this information, you can start the preparation for the elimination diet.

ELIMINATION DIET

Some of the most common foods that cause sensitivities include nightshade vegetables, nuts, wheat and other gluten-containing grains, dairy, soy and legumes, seafood, eggs, pork, and even citrus fruit. Some food types are obvious and easy to remove, but others can be a little more difficult, and parts of them (food components) may be found in other foods.

Before you can start to design your anti-inflammatory diet, you need to get rid of the foods that cause inflammation due to sensitivities, allergies, or intolerances. With the results of your allergen test, you will need five to six weeks to flush any traces of the food from your home and your body. There are four steps to the elimination diet.

Preparation	• Remove all the food and food components identified in the allergen test. • If you're sensitive to kale, you're likely to be sensitive to other cruciferous vegetables, such as broccoli or Brussels sprouts. • Read through the ingredient lists of packaged foods to determine if any food components (albumin found in eggs is also found in mayonnaise) may have been added and aren't obvious.

<table>
<tr><td>Elimination</td><td>

- For the next two to three weeks, ensure you don't eat anything on your allergen test until all your symptoms have disappeared.
- If symptoms continue, review the food you're eating to ensure the allergen or sensitivity isn't caused by a "hidden" ingredient in the ingredient list.
- This break allows the gut to recover from being overly sensitive to foods.

</td></tr>
<tr><td>Reintroduction</td><td>

- Once all symptoms of sensitivity have disappeared, start reintroducing the foods you have cut from your diet. This can take some time, depending on how many foods were cut out.
- Only reintroduce one food at a time over two to three days. Start with a teaspoon portion on the first day and wait for possible reactions. If there were no symptoms, double the portion the following day and double that the following day if there is no reaction. This food type shouldn't be eaten again until all the foods on the list have been reintroduced.
- Some reactions you can expect include rashes, bowel issues, headaches or migraines, stomach distress, fatigue, joint pain, and difficulty sleeping or breathing.
- If a reaction occurs during the reintroduction step, immediately stop eating the food that caused the reaction and don't test it again until all other foods needing reintroduction have been tested.
- Avoid introducing any foods until the symptoms subside.
- Continue to test all the foods until they have all been reintroduced or those that constantly cause reactions have been eliminated from your diet.

</td></tr>
</table>

<table>
<tr><td>Management</td><td>

- Once you know what you can and can't eat, it becomes easier to manage your diet, especially when testing new foods.
- In some cases, only part of a food type will cause a reaction, whereas others don't. Milk is a fine example. Some people with lactose intolerance can't handle milk at all, but they can still enjoy fermented versions of it, as the protein causing the reaction has been removed or denatured (broken down).

</td></tr>
</table>

Never add foods back into your diet if they have been classed as a food allergy. These foods will always have a chance of causing anaphylaxis which could result in death. However, don't give up hope of enjoying similar foods, as a variety of alternatives can be enjoyed.

When introducing new foods, ensure you add them to your food diary in great detail. Don't just say you had a pasta dish; make an effort to find out what went into making that dish so you can test each ingredient if you react to something.

BASIC GUIDELINES AND INGREDIENTS

Now that you know what shouldn't be in your unique diet, it's time to learn about the foods that should be added to an anti-inflammatory diet. The anti-inflammatory diet is all about getting as many vitamins, minerals, and nutrients from whole food as possible while avoiding eating foods such as refined carbohydrates and grains, processed meat, red meat, fried foods, and any foods with added sugar or salt. Ideally, you want to

- lower your added sugar intake

- increase foods with omega-3 fatty acids (nuts, seeds, and fatty fish)

- increase whole grains (avoiding any that contain gluten if you're gluten-sensitive)

- increase vegetable consumption, especially those that are considered dark green leafy vegetables

     The Science-Backed Anti-Inflammatory Diet for Beginners

- increase fruit consumption, preferably indulge in low-carbohydrate varieties, such as berries or tart cherries

- consume moderate levels of dairy, consuming the fermented variety for the extra probiotics

- avoid all processed foods

Fresh fruit and vegetables all offer polyphenols (a plant chemical) that are highly antioxidant and perfect for fighting against inflammation.

While prepackaged foods are a time-saver, they are often high in salt and made with refined grains, meaning they don't contain the fiber required by the gut microbiome to fight inflammation. Avoid these or make use of them infrequently. To help you make the right choices when it comes to choosing anti-inflammatory foods, here's a handy table.

Drinks	• Coffee contains polyphenols trigonelline, chlorogenic acid, and diterpenes that help to put a stop to damage caused by free radicals and lower the production of inflammatory compounds. • These benefits are best enjoyed with no added sugars and fats. • Green tea contains epigallocatechin-3-gallate, a powerful antioxidant, along with flavanols and polyphenols. Green tea is one of the healthiest drinks you can have.
Fruits	• Berries contain phytochemicals for fighting cancer development and progression, as well as the antioxidant anthocyanin for lowering inflammation. • Try combinations of strawberries, acai berries, blackberries, blueberries, raspberries, kiwi berries, and black currants.

- Avocado is high in fiber, good fats (monounsaturated), potassium, and magnesium. It also contains carotenoids and tocopherols, which help to lower the risk of cancer and heart disease.
- Grapes contain anthocyanins that help with decreasing inflammation and lower the risk of eye disorders, Alzheimer's disease, heart disease, obesity, and diabetes.
  - This fruit also contains resveratrol, a phenol known to protect the heart against inflammation. However, a supplement of resveratrol shows more promise than eating grapes.
- Cherries—especially tart cherries—have the antioxidant anthocyanins and catechins that combat inflammation.

Miscellaneous

- Cocoa and dark chocolate contain flavanols that lower inflammation and keep the lining of arteries healthy. It also assists in lowering blood pressure and reducing arterial stiffness.
  - When enjoying dark chocolate, ensure it's at least 70% cocoa.

Oils

- Extra virgin olive oil (EVOO) is high in monounsaturated fats, which help lower the risk of brain cancer, heart disease, obesity, and inflammatory markers.
  - It contains the antioxidant oleocanthal, which is considered to have the same level of anti-inflammatory properties as ibuprofen.
  - Ideally, use EVOO instead of other refined olive oils.

Omega-3 fatty acids	• The fattier the fish, the better. They are rich in eicosapentaenoic acid (EPA) and docosahexaenoic acid (DHA), two long-chain omega-3 fatty acids. · Not only do EPA and DHA lower inflammation, but when metabolized, they create protectins and resolvins, which also have anti-inflammatory effects. • Chia seeds are high in alpha-linolenic acid (ALA), a type of omega-3 fatty acid that can be converted to EPA and DHA within the body. Other foods that contain this include walnuts, soybeans, and flaxseeds.
Spices	• Turmeric contains curcumin, which is highly anti-inflammatory, lowering the inflammation associated with arthritis and diabetes. However, curcumin is poorly absorbed by the body. To improve absorption, this spice should be ingested with piperine found in black pepper. • There are no wrong herbs or spices! Experiment with all kinds to get an array of benefits, as most will help lower the action of the pro-inflammatory cytokines.
Whole grains	• Refined grains only contain the endosperm, which has some health benefits, but they offer more without being stripped of their germ and bran. · The bran and germ are rich in fiber, vitamins, minerals, and phytonutrients. The phenolic compounds suppress the production of pro-inflammatory compounds.
Vegetables	• All vegetables and culinary vegetables (tomatoes, peppers, etc.) contain antioxidants that assist in the decrease of inflammation. Aim to eat as many vegetables that are yellow, orange, red, and especially dark green.

- Broccoli contains the antioxidant sulforaphane, which lowers inflammation by combating nuclear factor kappa B (NF-kB) and cytokines. As with most cruciferous vegetables, broccoli helps with lowering the risk of cancer and heart disease.
- Hot and bell peppers are full of antioxidants and vitamin C. Bell peppers contain the antioxidant quercetin, which lowers the inflammation associated with many chronic diseases. Hot peppers contain sinapic acid and ferulic acid, which lowers inflammation and promotes healthier aging.
- Mushrooms are low in calories and contain all the B vitamins, as well as high levels of copper and selenium. This vegetable is high in phenols and antioxidants that give anti-inflammatory protection—especially against inflammatory bowel disease. Ensure that the mushrooms are only lightly cooked or enjoyed raw to get all the benefits.
- Tomatoes not only have high levels of potassium and vitamin C, but they are also packed with lycopene. Lycopene is highly anti-inflammatory, fighting against pro-inflammatory compounds that play roles in several cancers developing.
- Ideally, cook or eat tomatoes with olive oil to help absorb more lycopene.

Fruits often get a bad rap on diets due to their high sugar levels. While that can't be argued, different colored fruits should be included in your diet to ensure that you're getting all the nutrients and fiber required. As for fruit juice, this should be avoided as much as possible or watered down, as it's high in sugars (glucose), and without the fiber to slow down glucose digestion, it causes a spike in blood sugar.

While colorful vegetables are preferable, don't forget your starchy vegetables, such as legumes and potatoes, as they are high in nutrients, fiber, and resistant starches. Both are needed for your microbiome to keep you healthy. Note that if you have tested sensitive or allergic to anything on the list, it shouldn't be consumed.

A diet that works for you may not work for anyone else. This is why it's so important to individualize a diet, as this is how it can be successful! For this to work, you need to be honest with yourself about your eating habits and note foods that cause negative reactions.

Foods that cause allergies, intolerances, and sensitivities cause inflammation within your body, and they need to be eliminated from your diet before you can start adding all the new ingredients that align with the anti-inflammatory diet. The elimination diet will allow you to determine what is causing the problems in your current diet and will give you insight into what you can and can't eat from the list of anti-inflammatory foods.

Now that you have an understanding of putting your diet together and what equipment you can use to help you do it, it's time to delve into the scrumptious, decadent, and delectable recipes to get your morning started!

PART 2

THE ANTI-INFLAMMATORY COOKBOOK

Now is the time to gather the ingredients and equipment you need to put together breakfasts and brunches that will wow your friends and help lower chronic inflammation. Enjoy putting together quick smoothies and baked breakfasts that will encourage others to follow your new lifestyle without you ever having to say anything.

To help you find the recipes that are best suited to your needs, look out for the handy abbreviations that match your restrictions.

VG	Vegan-friendly
V	Vegetarian-friendly
DF	Dairy-free
GF	Gluten-free
EF	Egg-free
NF	Nut-free

Your taste and sensitivities aren't the same as others. So if you find an ingredient in a recipe that you react to, it's a good idea to seek alternatives that don't take away from the recipe. Here is a handy table with some examples to help you make choices regarding your unique sensitivities.

Added sugar	• Skip the various sugars in favor of pure stevia, monk fruit extract, maple syrup, or even coconut sugar.
Alcohol	• If you're cutting down on alcohol, consider substituting with low-sodium chicken or vegetable broth or alcohol-free dry white wine.
Animal-based meats	• If you're avoiding animal-based meats, turn to the recipes labeled as V or VG, or only use recipes from the plant-based section.

Dairy	• Dairy can be whole or low-fat. Where possible, aim to use low-fat.
	• Consider plant-based products made with almonds, oats, coconut, and so on.
	• There are a variety of milk, cheese, and yogurt that are plant-based.
	  · Always use varieties that don't have added sugar or use the phrase "sweetened."
	  · There are many plant-based options, so explore yogurts made from cashew, almond, and coconut. However, don't let this limit you! You can also enjoy low-fat yogurts or yogurts that are high in protein, such as Greek yogurt.

Eggs	• How an egg is replaced will depend on the recipe it is used in.
	  · With baking, mashed banana and apple sauce are often used. Generally, a quarter cup of puréed fruit is enough to replace one egg.
	  · When replacing eggs in a custard or pudding, a teaspoon of gelatin is enough for an egg.

Grains	• Many different gluten-free grains can be enjoyed, such as millet, barley, amaranth, rice, oats, quinoa, kamut, potato starch (thickening agent), cassava (flour), and oats.

	• However, there is a chance that people with gluten sensitivity may react to barley, kamut, and oats.
Soy	• Soy can be replaced with different kinds of beans, peas, lentils, chickpeas (garbanzo beans), carob, milk, or milk alternatives. • Soy sauce can be replaced with tamari sauce or coconut aminos.

All nutritional information provided with recipes is subject to change depending on substitutions.

CHAPTER 3:

BREAKFAST AND BRUNCH RECIPES

We as human beings have the amazing capacity to be reborn at breakfast every day and say, "This is a new day."
— Jack Kornfield

SMOOTHIES

Smoothies are the easiest and quickest way to get all the nutrients you need to jump-start your body for the day. It's also a great way to hide vegetables you would normally not want to eat due to their taste or texture. While smoothies are great and there are many different recipes, they don't last long. So if you plan to make a smoothie, you'll needv to enjoy it quickly after it's made. Thankfully, most recipes are as easy as throwing the ingredients into a blender and blending for about five minutes before your drink is ready to go with you as you step out the door for your day.

ALMOND BUTTER AND BANANA PROTEIN SMOOTHIE (V, VG, GF, EF, DF)

This smoothie has a natural sweet and nutty taste with the benefits of being high in protein, great for bone health while giving you a boost of fiber and vitamins C, K, and B9 (folate) along with an array of antioxidants.

Total Time: 5 minutes
Serving Size: 1
Prep Time: 5 minutes
Cook Time: no cooking required
Nutritional Facts:
per recipe
Calories: 402 kcal
Carbs: 37 g
Fat: 22 g
Protein: 19 g

Ingredients:

- ½ tsp ground cinnamon
- 1 cup unsweetened almond milk
- 1 small frozen banana, chopped
- 2 tbsp protein powder of choice
- 2 tbsp almond butter
- 4–6 ice cubes
- 1 tbsp sweetener of choice (optional)

Directions:

1. Add all the ingredients into the blender, and blend on high until smooth.

RASPBERRY–PEACH–MANGO SMOOTHIE BOWL (V, GF, EF)

There's nothing better on a hot morning than a brightly colored, fruit-packed smoothie bowl. This creamy, frosty, edible smoothie allows you to enjoy your morning with some mindful eating, allowing you to start your day with a boost of antioxidants from the berries.

Total Time: 10 minutes
Serving Size: 1
Prep Time: 10 minutes
Cook Time: no cooking required
Nutritional Facts: per recipe
Calories: 352 kcal
Carbs: 46 g
Fat: 9 g
Protein: 23 g

Ingredients:

- ¼ cup reduced-fat milk
- ¼ ripe peach, sliced
- ⅓ cup fresh raspberries
- ¾ cup unsweetened cashew yogurt
- 1 tbsp sliced almonds
- 1 cup frozen mango, cut into chunks
- 1 tbsp unsweetened coconut flakes
- 1 tsp vanilla extract
- 1 tsp chia seeds

Directions:

1. To a blender, add the milk, mango, vanilla, and banana, then blend until smooth.
2. Pour the purée mixture into a bowl and scatter in the remaining ingredients to taste.

PEANUT BUTTER AND JELLY SMOOTHIE (V, EF, GF)

Everyone loves the taste of a PB&J sandwich but don't have the time to put it together. Turn this classic sandwich into a drink and enjoy the boost of calcium, fiber, and protein. Hide the taste of the spinach or kale behind the sweet banana to get your greens for the morning.

Total Time: 5 minutes
Serving Size: 1
Prep Time: 5 minutes
Cook Time: no cooking required
Nutritional Facts: per recipe
Calories: 367 kcal
Carbs: 54 g
Fat: 10 g
Protein: 18 g

Ingredients:

- ⅓ cup nonfat plain Greek yogurt
- ½ cup low-fat milk
- ½ cup frozen strawberries
- 1 cup frozen banana slices
- 1 cup baby spinach or kale
- 1 tbsp natural almond butter
- 1–2 tsp maple syrup or manuka honey (optional)

Directions:

1. To a blender, add the yogurt and milk, followed by the remaining ingredients.
2. Blend on high until smooth.

The Science-Backed Anti-Inflammatory Diet for Beginners

MANGO–ALMOND SMOOTHIE BOWL (V, EF, GF)

Smoothie bowls are highly adaptable to what you need to give you a boost in the morning. This thick and creamy bowl is perfect for your heart, and the addition of unsalted almonds will help reduce your blood sugar, blood pressure, and cholesterol.

Total Time: 10 minutes
Serving Size: 1
Prep Time: 10 minutes
Cook Time: no cooking required
Nutritional Facts:
per recipe
Calories: 457 kcal
Carbs: 46 g
Fat: 24 g
Protein: 22 g

Ingredients:

- ⅛ tsp ground allspice
- ¼ cup plain unsweetened almond milk
- ¼ cup fresh raspberries
- ¼ cup frozen banana, sliced
- ½ cup nonfat plain Greek yogurt
- ½ cup frozen mango, chopped
- ½ tsp manuka honey
- 5 tbsp unsalted almonds, divided

Directions:

1. To make the smoothie, add the allspice, mango, banana, 3 tablespoons of almonds, almond milk, and yogurt until well combined.
2. Pour the mixture into a bowl and add the remaining almonds and the fresh raspberries before drizzling the honey over everything before serving.

BERRY–KEFIR SMOOTHIE (V, VG, EF, DF, GF)

Kefir is one of the best foods you can add to your diet. It's a nutrient-dense, fermented milk drink that's a powerful probiotic, even more than yogurt! It's great for improving not only your gut health but also your bone health and is gentler for those who are lactose intolerant.

Total Time: 5 minutes
Serving Size: 1
Prep Time: 5 minutes
Cook Time: no cooking required
Nutritional Facts:
per recipe
Calories: 304 kcal
Carbs: 53 g
Fat: 7 g
Protein: 15 g

Ingredients:

- ½ medium banana
- ½ tsp vanilla extract
- 1 cup plain kefir
- 1 ½ cups frozen mixed berries
- 2 tsp almond butter
- some chia seeds (optional)

Directions:

1. Add all ingredients to the blender and blend until smooth.
2. Sprinkle the optional chia seeds before serving to add extra fiber.

BLACKBERRY SMOOTHIE (V, GF, EF, NF)

Blackberries not only give this smoothie a beautiful color, but they're rich in vitamins C and K, manganese, and fiber. Add a touch of honey if you find the smoothie too sour.

Total Time: 5 minutes
Serving Size: 1
Prep Time: 5 minutes
Cook Time: no cooking required
Nutritional Facts:
per recipe
Calories: 316 kcal
Carbs: 53 g
Fat: 7 g
Protein: 15 g

Ingredients:

- ½ cup plain nonfat Greek yogurt
- ½ medium banana
- 1 tbsp manuka honey
- 1 cup (6 oz) fresh or frozen blackberries
- 1 tsp fresh ginger, finely chopped
- 1 ½ tsp fresh lemon juice

Directions:

1. Add all the ingredients to a blender and blend for 2 minutes before serving.

SPINACH–AVOCADO SMOOTHIE (V, NF, GF, EG)

Not everyone loves spinach, but this smoothie is sure to change your mind! With the delicate and creamy nature of avocado and the natural sweetness of banana, this smoothie will jump-start your energy.

Total Time: 5 minutes
Serving Size: 1
Prep Time: 5 minutes
Cook Time: no cooking required
Nutritional Facts:
per recipe
Calories: 357 kcal
Carbs: 58 g
Fat: 8 g
Protein: 18 g

Ingredients:

- ¼ avocado
- 1 cup fresh spinach
- 1 cup nonfat plain Greek yogurt
- 1 frozen medium banana
- 2 tbsp water or 1–2 ice cubes
- 1 tsp manuka honey (optional)

Directions:

1. Blend all ingredients in a blender until smooth.

REALLY GREEN SMOOTHIE (V, VG, GF, EF, DF)

With the bitterness of kale hidden behind creamy avocado, this is a smoothie you may struggle to stay away from. With the boost in vitamins A, B9 (folate), C, and K, along with minerals zinc, phosphorus, magnesium, and calcium, you'll be starting your morning with all the nutrients needed to get to lunch.

Total Time: 5 minutes

Serving Size: 1

Prep Time: 5 minutes

Cook Time: no cooking required

Nutritional Facts:
per recipe
Calories: 343 kcal
Carbs: 55 g
Fat: 14 g
Protein: 6 g

Ingredients:

- ¼ ripe avocado
- 1 cup ice cubes
- 1 large ripe banana
- 1 cup unsweetened vanilla almond milk
- 1 tbsp chia seeds
- 1 cup packed baby kale
- 2 tsp manuka honey

Directions:

1. Add all ingredients, except the ice cubes, and blend until smooth.
2. Then include the ice cubes and blend until the mixture is well combined.

CARROT–APPLE SMOOTHIE (DF, V, VG, GF, EF)

This smoothie is reminiscent of a tropical holiday. The carrots and apples bring not only a natural sweetness, but they are full of fiber, vitamins, and minerals, which help with lowering cholesterol, inflammation, and the risk of heart disease and boosting eye health.

Total Time: 5 minutes
Serving Size: 2
Prep Time: 5 minutes
Cook Time: no cooking required
Nutritional Facts:
per serving
Calories: 243 kcal
Carbs: 46 g
Fat: 8 g
Protein: 4 g

Ingredients:

- ½ cup ice cubes
- 1 large Honeycrisp apple, cored and quartered
- 1 medium ripe banana
- 1 cup light coconut milk
- 2 large (or 1 ½ cups) carrots, sliced
- 1 tsp ground turmeric or 2 tsp fresh turmeric, minced
- 2 tsp fresh ginger, minced
- 2 tbsp fresh lemon juice

Directions:

1. Add all the ingredients except the ice cubes and blend for 45 seconds.
2. Include the ice cubes before blending for another 30 seconds.

MIXED BERRY BREAKFAST SMOOTHIE (V, GF, EF)

With all the benefits of berries, it can be difficult to pick just one type, so don't. Berries are known for their fiber, minerals potassium and magnesium, and vitamins C and K. Together with avocado and walnuts, you'll have enough healthy fats to see you to your next meal.

Total Time: 5 minutes
Serving Size: 1
Prep Time: 5 minutes
Cook Time: no cooking required
Nutritional Facts:
per recipe
Calories: 424 kcal
Carbs: 55 g
Fat: 21 g
Protein: 17 g

Ingredients:

- ¼ avocado
- ½ cup low-fat plain Greek yogurt
- ¾ cup water
- 1 cup frozen mixed berries
- 1 medium banana
- 2 tbsp walnuts, chopped

Directions:

1. Blend all ingredients on high until smooth.
2. If the consistency is too thick, add a few teaspoons of water, adding a teaspoon at a time.

EGGS AND GRAINS

Most people like to start their day with a hearty breakfast containing eggs, grains, or even a combination of both. Eggs and grains are powerhouses of energy and will not only keep you fuller for longer but come with many benefits.

Eggs	• Eggs contain 13 vitamins, minerals, omega-3 fatty acids, antioxidants, and protein.
	• Eggs contain all the essential amino acids needed to help with muscle movement, growth, and recovery.
	• They have high-density lipoprotein, also known as the "good" cholesterol.
	• Two eggs' worth of yolks is almost enough to cover the required daily dose of vitamin D.
	• They contain choline, which is required by the body for normal cell function and helps with the development of the spinal cord, brain, and cognition. It also reduces cognitive decline in the elderly.
	• Egg antioxidants help protect your eyes against degeneration of vision associated with age. · The antioxidants lutein and zeaxanthin help protect against cataract development and macular degeneration.
	• Eggs can even help support mental health as vitamins B2 and B12, with iron, tryptophan, and choline, help lower the risk of anxiety, improve sleep, and lower the symptoms of depression.
	• Having eggs for breakfast is great, as they contain the hormone ghrelin, which helps you feel satiated. Eggs also help increase metabolic activity and slow the rate at which food leaves the stomach, allowing for better digestion.

<table>
<tr><td>

Grains

</td><td>

- Whole grains are grains that haven't had their bran and germ stripped to make refined grains, which only contain the endosperm.
- The bran and germ contain most vitamins, minerals, and antioxidants.
  - The bran is full of fiber, B-complex, and minerals iron, copper, magnesium, and zinc, along with antioxidants and phytochemicals.
  - The germ is nutrient-packed with the vitamins B-complex and E, along with antioxidants, phytochemicals, and healthy fats.
- The bran and germ are high in fiber, which slows down the digestion of the endosperm, helping to maintain blood sugar levels.
  - The fiber also helps to lower cholesterol, moving solid waste from the body and lowering the chance of blood clots developing.

</td></tr>
</table>

LEMON–BERRY RICOTTA TOAST (EF, V, NF)

Ricotta is a type of cheese with a mild, almost grainy, taste that brings a creamy texture to a zesty, sweet, and tart breakfast all rolled into one meal.

Total Time: 10 minutes
Serving Size: 2
Prep Time: 10 minutes
Cook Time: no cooking required
Nutritional Facts: per serving
Calories: 162 kcal
Carbs: 22 g
Fat: 5 g
Protein: 7 g

Ingredients:

- ¼ cup whole milk ricotta cheese
- ½ tsp lemon zest, plus an extra ¼ tsp for topping
- ½ cup fresh berries of choice
- 2 tsp maple syrup
- 2 slices whole-grain bread, toasted

Directions:

1. In a small bowl, mix ½ teaspoon lemon zest, maple syrup, and ricotta until well combined.
2. Divide the mixture in two and spread on the toast.
3. Top each slice with ¼ cup berries and ⅛ of lemon zest before serving.

SPINACH AND MUSHROOM EGG BITES (V, GF, NF)

While this breakfast may take a little longer than others, it'll be well worth it, as these egg bites can last up to three days in the fridge or three months in the freezer. Remember to wrap individually before freezing.

Total Time: 50 minutes
Serving Size: 6
Prep Time: 15 minutes
Cook Time: 35 minutes
Nutritional Facts:
per serving
Calories: 159 kcal
Carbs: 4 g
Fat: 10 g
Protein: 13 g

Ingredients:

- ¼ cup shredded Swiss cheese
- ½ tsp black pepper
- ½ tsp salt, divided
- ¾ cup nonfat cottage cheese
- 1 tbsp EVOO
- 1 ½ cups cremini mushrooms, sliced
- 2 cups water, boiled
- 3 cups packed baby spinach
- 8 large eggs

Directions:

1. Preheat the oven to 350 °F.
2. Prepare the 12-cup silicone muffin pan with cooking spray.
3. In a large pan, over medium heat, heat the oil before adding the mushrooms. Cook for 6–8 minutes or until brown.
4. Add the spinach to the mushrooms and cook for a minute allowing leaves to wilt. Stir in half the salt, and allow the mixture to cool for 5 minutes.
5. Place the cooled mixture into a food processor and pulse until the mixture is finely chopped.
6. Add a tablespoon of the chopped vegetables to the muffin cups before cleaning the food processor.
7. To the clean food processor, add the remaining salt, pepper, eggs, and cottage cheese, and blend on medium until smooth.
8. Add the Swiss cheese and pulse until it is incorporated with the egg mixture.
9. Pour ¼ cup of the mixture into each muffin cup.
10. Take the muffin tray and place it in a larger baking tray and fill it with 2 cups of boiled water.
11. Bake the egg bites for 25 minutes or until set.
12. Allow the bites to cool for 5 minutes before serving or store them for later enjoyment.

ALMOND FLOUR PANCAKES (DF, GF, V, VG)

Pancakes can also be enjoyed by those who have gluten sensitivities or intolerances. These delicious almond pancakes are light and fluffy and can be topped with just about everything.

Total Time: 15 minutes
Serving Size: 2
Prep Time: 5 minutes
Cook Time: 10 minutes
Nutritional Facts:
per recipe
Calories: 354 kcal
Carbs: 25 g
Fat: 23 g
Protein: 17 g

Ingredients:

- ⅓ cup coconut milk
- 1 cup almond flour
- 2 tbsp maple syrup
- 2 tsp coconut oil, for cooking
- 2 eggs
- sea salt, to taste

Directions:

1. Mix all ingredients, except the coconut oil, in a large bowl until a batter is formed.
2. Add the coconut oil to a skillet and add it to medium heat.
3. Use a ¼ cup to pour batter into the skillet.
4. Allow the batter to cook for 3 minutes or until bubbles appear on the surface. Flip and allow to cook for another 2–3 minutes.
5. Serve with preferred toppings.

BREAKFAST BURRITOS (V, NF)

These breakfast burritos only take 30 minutes to make and can last three months frozen, making them ideal to grab on your way out! Not only are they delicious with their spicy and cheesy bite, but they are highly adaptable, so experiment with different cheeses and vegetables.

Total Time: 30 minutes
Serving Size: 6
Prep Time: 20 minutes
Cook Time: 10 minutes
Nutritional Facts:
per serving
Calories: 297 kcal
Carbs: 20 g
Fat: 15 g
Protein: 19 g

Ingredients:

- ¼ tsp ground pepper
- ¼ tsp salt
- ½ cup pepper Jack cheese, shredded
- ½ tsp paprika
- 1 tbsp serrano pepper, deseeded and chopped finely
- 2 cups baby spinach
- 2 tsp EVOO
- 6 (8-inch) whole wheat tortillas
- 12 large eggs

Directions:

1. In a large pan, heat some oil over medium-low heat.
2. Add the paprika and serrano peppers to cook for 1–2 minutes.
3. Place the spinach in the pan and cook until just wilted.
4. Crack in the eggs and mix occasionally while they cook for 5 minutes or until mostly set.
5. Lay out the tortillas on their own sheet of foil before adding ½ cup of the scrambled eggs to the lower half of the tortilla.
6. Divide the cheese between the tortillas and roll them, remembering to tuck in the ends.
7. Wrap the entire tortilla in foil if freezing, or enjoy immediately.
8. To reheat the tortilla, remove the foil, add it to a microwave-safe plate, and cook on medium for 1–2 minutes, followed by cooking on high for 1–2 minutes.
9. Alternatively, keep the foil on and bake in the oven for 25 minutes at 375 °F.

BAKED OATMEAL (V, GF, EF)

Oatmeal doesn't need to be boring, especially when you play around with natural sweeteners such as bananas and raisins. If you enjoy a warm breakfast that doesn't involve eggs, then this should be your go-to recipe. Check that your oatmeal is gluten-free..

Total Time: 1 hour
Serving Size: 6
Prep Time: 10 minutes
Cook Time: 50 minutes
Nutritional Facts:
per serving
Calories: 327 kcal
Carbs: 46 g
Fat: 13 g
Protein: 9 g

Ingredients:

- ¼ tsp ground allspice
- ¼ cup packed coconut palm sugar
- ⅓ cup walnuts, chopped
- ⅓ cup raisins
- ½ tsp salt
- ¾ cup plain Greek yogurt
- 1 tsp baking powder
- 1 large banana, halved lengthwise and sliced
- 1 tsp vanilla extract
- 1 ½ tsp ground cinnamon
- 2 tbsp EVOO
- 2 cups rolled oats
- 2 cups almond milk

Directions:

1. Preheat the oven to 375 °F.
2. Spray the inside of an 8-inch baking dish with cooking spray.
3. In a large bowl, add the allspice, oats, salt, baking powder, walnuts, and cinnamon, and mix well.
4. In a secondary bowl, pour in the yogurt, milk, vanilla, sugar, and oil, and stir until the sugar dissolves.
5. Pour the milk mixture into the dry ingredients until everything is well incorporated.
6. Scatter the raisins and banana, then stir before pouring into the baking dish.
7. Bake for 45–50 minutes or until the top turns golden brown and is firm to touch.

   The Science-Backed Anti-Inflammatory Diet for Beginners

GOURMET AVOCADO TOAST (V, DF, NF)

Move aside avocado and toast and move over for the glammed-up version! The eggs add the protein, the spinach the fiber, the avocado the creamy healthy fat, and the salsa the heat—everything you need in a breakfast.

Total Time: 13 minutes
Serving Size: 1
Prep Time: 5 minutes
Cook Time: 8 minutes
Nutritional Facts:
per recipe
Calories: 364 kcal
Carbs: 24 g
Fat: 26 g
Protein: 14 g

Ingredients:

- ½ small avocado, mashed
- 1 tbsp salsa
- 1 clove garlic, minced
- 1 slice whole-grain bread, toasted
- 1 large egg
- 1 tsp EVOO, divided
- 2 cups baby spinach
- a pinch of ground pepper

Directions:

1. Add the avocado to the toast, and season to preference.
2. In a skillet, heat ½ teaspoon of oil over medium heat.
3. Add the spinach and garlic and cook for a minute; it should just be wilted. Place on top of the toast.
4. Add the remaining oil to the skillet and add the egg to cook over medium-low heat for 5–7 minutes, if you like soft yolks. If you like harder yolks, cook for 1–2 minutes longer.
5. Place the eggs on the spinach and top with salsa before serving.

LEMON–BLUEBERRY YOGURT TOAST (V, NF)

With a unique mixture of yogurt and eggs resulting in a creamy, tasty mixture similar to Danish cheese, this quick morning meal will give you the taste sensation you were dreaming about!

Total Time: 20 minutes
Serving Size: 2
Prep Time: 5 minutes
Cook Time: 15 minutes
Nutritional Facts:
per serving
Calories: 167 kcal
Carbs: 23 g
Fat: 5 g
Protein: 9 g

Ingredients:

- ¼ cup fresh blueberries
- 1 tbsp pure maple syrup
- 1 tsp lemon juice
- 1 large egg
- 1 tsp lemon zest
- 2 slices whole wheat bread, cut to ½-inch thick
- 3 tbsp plain whole milk Greek yogurt
- a pinch of salt

Directions:

1. Preheat the oven to 375 °F.
2. Line your baking sheet with parchment paper and set aside.
3. In a small bowl, add all the ingredients, other than the bread, and whisk well.
4. Add the bread slices to the baking sheet and create an indent in the center of the bread that is big enough to leave a ½-inch border between it and the crust.
5. Pour the yogurt mixture into the indent and even it before topping with blueberries.
6. Bake for 8–10 minutes until the yogurt mixture is set.
7. Allow to cool for 5 minutes before enjoying.

CHICKPEA OMELET (DF, EF, V, VG, NF, GF)

A clever mixture of chickpea flour and kala namak (black salt) produces an omelet-like mixture with a creamy, custard-like center with a light and fluffy exterior. Black salt has long been used in Ayurveda cooking and healing and is used to aid digestion while fighting against constipation, bloating, and indigestion.

Total Time: 20 minutes
Serving Size: 1
Prep Time: 10 minutes
Cook Time: 10 minutes
Nutritional Facts:
per recipe
Calories: 250 kcal
Carbs: 19 g
Fat: 16 g
Protein: 8 g

Ingredients:

- ⅛ tsp kala namak
- ⅛ tsp ground turmeric
- ¼ tsp baking powder
- ⅛ tsp onion powder
- ⅛ tsp garlic powder
- ⅓ cup water
- ⅓ cup chickpea flour
- 1 tbsp EVOO, divided
- 1 ½ tsp nutritional yeast
- herbs of choice

Optional Fillings (choose one from the three)
- ¾ cup mixed cooked vegetables (such as bell peppers, onions, or mushrooms)
- ¾ cup vegan or regular cheese of choice
- ¾ cup vegan meat substitute

Directions:

1. Keeping 1 ½ tsp of oil aside for cooking, add all other ingredients to a bowl and whisk until smooth. Let the mixture stand for 5 minutes.
2. Pour the remaining oil into a skillet and heat over medium, ensuring the pan is coated before pouring in the batter.
3. Leave the batter to cook for 4 minutes undisturbed. The top should look dry with bubbles before removing from heat.
4. Add any additional fillings you want and fold the omelet closed.
5. Place a lid on the pan and allow the omelet to steam for a further 5 minutes.

AVOCADO AND SMOKED SALMON OMELET (GF, NF)

Not only is this recipe high in good fats and omega-3 fatty acids, but if you're on a keto or low-calorie diet, then this breakfast is for you! If sensitive to smoked salmon, use cooked fresh salmon instead.

Total Time: 10 minutes
Serving Size: 1
Prep Time: 5 minutes
Cook Time: 5 minutes
Nutritional Facts:
per recipe
Calories: 323 kcal
Carbs: 5 g
Fat: 25 g
Protein: 19 g

Ingredients:

- ¼ avocado, sliced
- 1 tbsp chopped fresh basil
- 1 tsp low-fat milk
- 1 oz smoked salmon
- 1 ½ tsp EVOO, divided
- 2 large eggs
- a pinch of salt

Directions:

1. In a small bowl, beat the salt, milk, and eggs.
2. Heat a teaspoon of oil over medium heat before adding the egg mixture.
3. Cook the mixture for 1–2 minutes. The bottom should be set and the center a little runny.
4. Flip the omelet and cook for 30 seconds before plating.
5. Top with avocado, basil, and salmon before drizzling the remaining oil over the meal.

STRAWBERRY YOGURT PARFAIT (V, GF, EF, NF)

Nothing is better than fresh, juicy fruit with the tartness of yogurt and the granola crunch. A mixture of all three brings you the parfait that is easy to make and greatly enjoyed afterward. Lower your sugar intake by squashing the fruit a little instead of adding sugar.

Total Time: 10 minutes

Serving Size: 1

Prep Time: 10 minutes

Cook Time: no cooking required

Nutritional Facts:
per recipe
Calories: 285 kcal
Carbs: 37 g
Fat: 8 g
Protein: 17 g

Ingredients:

- ¼ cup homemade granola (rolled oats, coconut oil, some cinnamon baked in the oven, or sugar-free granola)
- ½ cup nonfat Greek yogurt
- 1 tsp stevia
- 1 cup fresh strawberries, sliced

Directions:

1. In a small bowl, add the strawberries and sprinkle the sugar over to aid in releasing juice. Set aside for 5 minutes.
2. In a mason jar, layer the granola, yogurt, and strawberry mixture. Top with a sprinkle of granola.

QUICK BITES

While breakfast is seen by many as the most important meal of the day, some people can't stomach a large meal early in the day. If you're one of these people, have a sneak peek at the quick bites below that will still fuel your day but won't make you feel overfull.

BANANA MUFFINS (GF, DF, VG, EF, V)

Instead of saving those mushy bananas for banana bread, use them for muffins. Consider adding some cocoa nibs to enhance the muffins to your preferred taste.

Total Time: 35 minutes
Serving Size: 6
Prep Time: 10 minutes
Cook Time: 25 minutes
Nutritional Facts:
per serving
Calories: 178 kcal
Carbs: 38 g
Fat: 3 g
Protein: 4 g

Ingredients:

- ¼ tsp salt
- ¼ tsp baking soda
- ½ tbsp apple cider vinegar
- ½ tsp ground ginger
- ½ cup unsweetened vanilla almond milk
- ¾ cup ripe banana, mashed
- ¾ cup dates, halved and tightly packed
- 1 tsp vanilla extract
- 1 tsp baking powder
- 1 cup oat flour
- 1 ½ tsp curcumin powder
- 2 tbsp cocoa nibs

Directions:

1. Preheat the oven to 400 °F and prepare a 6-well muffin pan with cooking spray.

2. Add the vanilla, dates, apple cider vinegar, milk, and banana to a food processor, and blend until smooth. Scrape the sides, if necessary.

3. Place the remaining ingredients, except the cocoa

nibs, in a large bowl and mix until well incorporated.

4. Pour the dry ingredients into the food processor and blend until smooth. Scrape sides as needed.
5. Pour the batter into the large bowl and fold in the cocoa nibs.
6. Split the batter between the wells of the muffin pan and bake for 20–25 minutes. Ensure that an inserted toothpick to the center of a muffin comes out clean.
7. Allow muffins to cool for 10 minutes in the pan before transferring to a cooling rack.

BREAKFAST SALAD (GF, V, NF)

A breakfast salad is the best way to get most of your vegetables consumed early in the day. However, be warned that not everyone likes fresh cilantro (the leaves of the coriander plant), as it can taste like soap to some.

Total Time: 10 minutes

Serving Size: 1

Prep Time: 10 minutes

Cook Time: no cooking required

Nutritional Facts: per recipe

Calories: 527 kcal

Carbs: 37 g

Fat: 34 g

Protein: 16 g

Ingredients:

- ¼ avocado, sliced
- ½ cup canned red kidney beans, rinsed
- 1 tbsp plus 1 tsp EVOO, divided
- 1 large egg
- 2 cups salad greens
- 2 tbsp chopped cilantro, plus more for garnish
- 3 tbsp salsa verde
- 8 blue corn tortilla chips, broken into large pieces (optional)

Directions:

1. In a small bowl, add the cilantro, salsa, and a tablespoon of oil, then whisk.
2. Pour half the mixture over the greens in a shallow bowl.
3. To the salad, layer the avocado, chips, and beans.
4. Add a skillet to medium heat and heat the remaining oil before frying the egg for 2 minutes or until preferred doneness.
5. Place the egg on the salad and drizzle with the remaining dressing with a sprinkle of extra cilantro.

SPINACH AND FETA SCRAMBLED EGG PITAS (NF, V)

Pitas are a great way to grab a meal and eat it on the move, and they can be filled with so many healthy ingredients. If you prefer warm pitas before filling them, wrap them in foil and place them in an oven at 350 °F for 8–10 minutes.

Total Time: 15 minutes
Serving Size: 4
Prep Time: 5 minutes
Cook Time: 10 minutes
Nutritional Facts:
per serving
Calories: 303 kcal
Carbs: 21 g
Fat: 16 g
Protein: 20 g

Ingredients:

- ¼ cup feta cheese, crumbled finely
- 1 (10 oz) block of frozen chopped spinach, thawed, drained, and squeezed dry (or 1 lb of fresh spinach)
- 1 tbsp EVOO
- 4 (5-inch) whole wheat or gluten-free pitas, cut in half
- 8 tsp sun-dried tomato pesto
- 8 large eggs, beaten
- freshly ground pepper to taste
- a pinch of salt

Directions:

1. Place a skillet over medium heat and heat the oil before adding the spinach and the salt, cooking until it starts to wilt, stirring occasionally.
2. Pour in the eggs and stir lightly for 4–5 minutes to create soft curds.
3. Add the pepper and feta and allow the eggs to cook until set.
4. Spread 2 teaspoons of pesto thinly to the insides of each pita half before dividing the cooked mixture between them.

AVOCADO AND SMOKED TROUT BREAKFAST SALAD (GF, DF, EG, NF)

Trout is high in omega-3 fatty acids and vitamins B6, B12, and B3 (niacin). Together with avocado, this meal ticks all the boxes for the necessary fiber, protein, and healthy fats. Duis aute irure dolor in reprehenderit in voluptate velit esse cillum dolore eu fugiat nulla pariatur.

Total Time: 10 minutes
Serving Size: 1
Prep Time: 10 minutes
Cook Time: no cooking required
Nutritional Facts:
per recipe
Calories: 275 kcal

Carbs: 9 g

Fat: 23 g

Protein: 10 g

Ingredients:

- ¼ firm ripe avocado, sliced
- ¼ cup smoked trout, flaked
- 1 tsp minced garlic
- 1 tbsp red onion, finely chopped

- 1 tbsp EVOO
- 2 tsp red wine vinegar
- 3 cups lightly packed baby kale
- a pinch of salt
- a pinch of pepper

Directions:

1. Create a salt and garlic paste by mashing them together.
2. In a medium bowl, whisk the garlic paste, pepper, vinegar, and oil.
3. Add the kale and toss lightly before topping with red onion, avocado, and trout.

HONEY-ROASTED CHERRY AND RICOTTA TARTINE (EF, V)

A tartine is a bread slice topped with something sweet or savory. With this tartine, the creaminess of the thyme-spiked ricotta pairs well with either sweet or tart cherries. The roasted cherries can be prepared three days in advance and stored in the fridge. Remember to reheat before use.

Total Time: 25 minutes
Serving Size: 4
Prep Time: 10 minutes
Cook Time: 15 minutes
Nutritional Facts:
per serving
Calories: 320 kcal
Carbs: 40 g
Fat: 13 g
Protein: 15 g

Ingredients:

- ¼ cup slivered almonds, toasted
- 1 tbsp manuka honey, plus
- extra for serving
- 1 tbsp lemon juice
- 1 tsp fresh thyme

- 1 tsp lemon zest
- 1 cup part-skim ricotta cheese
- 2 tsp EVOO
- 2 cups pitted fresh cherries
- 4 whole-grain artisan bread, cut to ½-inch thick
- a pinch of salt
- a pinch of flaky sea salt

Directions:

1. Preheat the oven to 400 °F.
2. Place parchment paper on a baking sheet.
3. In a bowl, mix the cherries with salt, oil, lemon juice, and honey before adding to the sheet.
4. Allow the cherries to cook for 15 minutes, shaking the baking sheet once or twice.
5. Toast the bread before topping with thyme, ricotta, sea salt, almonds, cooked cherries, and lemon zest.

FANCY EGG SANDWICHES (V, NF)

Enjoy this classic egg sandwich with a Mediterranean twist, bursting with flavor. If you can't find sandwich thins, substitute with multigrain English muffins.

Total Time: 15 minutes
Serving Size: 4
Prep Time: 5 minutes
Cook Time: 10 minutes
Nutritional Facts:
per serving
Calories: 242 kcal
Carbs: 25 g
Fat: 12 g
Protein: 13 g

Ingredients:

- ⅛ tsp salt
- 1 tbsp fresh or ½ tsp dried rosemary leaves, crushed
- 1 medium tomato, cut into 8 thin slices

- 2 cups fresh baby spinach
- 4 multigrain sandwich thins
- 4 tbsp reduced-fat feta cheese
- 4 tsp EVOO
- 4 eggs
- freshly ground black pepper

Directions:

1. Preheat the oven to 375 °F.
2. Cut the thins open, brush the insides with 2 teaspoons of olive oil, and add to a baking sheet before toasting for 5 minutes. The edges should be crisp and light brown.
3. Heat the remaining oil in a skillet on high heat, then add the eggs and cook to preferred doneness. Flip, if you like, before removing from the heat.
4. Add the toasted bread to four plates. To one slice, add the spinach, two tomato slices, and an egg, and sprinkle a tablespoon of feta over.
5. Season to taste and close the sandwich.

DATE AND PINE NUT OVERNIGHT OATS
(VG, V, DF, GF, EF)

Having overnight oats is a great way to create a scrumptious breakfast the night before that doesn't take much time and is adaptable.

Total Time: 8 hours

Serving Size: 1

Prep Time: 10 minutes

Cook Time: no cooking required but allow the oats to rest overnight

Nutritional Facts:
per recipe

Calories: 282 kcal

Carbs: 48 g

Fat: 9 g

Protein: 7 g

The Science-Backed Anti-Inflammatory Diet for Beginners

Ingredients:

- ¼ tsp ground cinnamon
- ½ cup water
- ½ cup old-fashioned rolled oats
- 1 tsp manuka honey
- 1 tbsp toasted pine nuts
- 2 tbsp chopped dates
- a pinch of salt

Directions:

1. In a jar or bowl, add the salt, water, and oats, stir, cover, and leave in the fridge overnight.
2. When you're ready to eat, top with the remaining ingredients and enjoy.

CHEESY GREEN FRITTATA (GF, V, NF)

Frittatas are similar to omelets, but instead of folding them over, they are open-faced. This particular frittata uses basil, which contains eugenol, an antioxidant that is highly anti-inflammatory in the digestive tract.

Total Time: 20 minutes
Serving Size: 4
Prep Time: 5 minutes
Cook Time: 15 minutes
Nutritional Facts:
per serving
Calories: 292 kcal
Carbs: 8 g
Fat: 21 g
Protein: 18 g

Ingredients:

- ¼ cup fresh basil, thinly sliced
- ¼ tsp freshly ground pepper
- ½ tsp salt
- 1 ½ cups zucchini, chopped
- 1 ½ cups red onion, thinly sliced
- 2 tbsp EVOO
- 3 tbsp soft sun-dried tomatoes, chopped
- 4 oz baby fresh mozzarella balls
- 7 large eggs, beaten

Directions:

1. Preheat the broiler (500 °F) for 5–10 minutes, setting the position rack in the upper third of the oven.
2. Over medium-high heat, heat the oil in the oven-safe skillet. Add the zucchini and onion and cook for 3–5 minutes, stirring until soft.
3. Whisk the pepper, salt, and eggs in a bowl before pouring over the skillet's contents.
4. While the egg mixture is cooking, lift the edges to allow the runny mixture to flow under and cook.
5. Cook for 2 minutes before scattering the tomatoes and mozzarella onto the mixture and placing the skillet in the oven.
6. Allow the mixture to cook for 1 ½–2 minutes or until it starts to brown. Remove from the oven.
7. Allow the frittata to cool for 3 minutes before adding the fresh basil.
8. Use a spatula to loosen the edges and bottom of the frittata before portioning it and serving.

QUINOA AND CHIA OATMEAL MIX (EF, V, VG, NF, DF)

This oatmeal mixture can be prepared and stored for up to a month, allowing you to partake in it whenever you wish. Quinoa is often overlooked as a grain, but it's worth eating, as it's great for getting your boost of vitamin B9, magnesium, iron, and potassium.

Total Time: 20 minutes
Serving Size: 4
Prep Time: 5 minutes
Cook Time: 15 minutes
Nutritional Facts:
per serving
Calories: 292 kcal
Carbs: 8 g
Fat: 21 g
Protein: 18 g

Ingredients:

- ½ cup chia or hempseeds
- ¾ tsp salt
- 1 cup rolled wheat or barley flakes or a mixture of both
- 1 cup dried fruits (raisins, cranberries, chopped apricots, etc.)
- 1 tsp ground cinnamon
- 1 cup quinoa
- 2 cups rolled oats

Directions:

1. Start with the dry mix by adding all the ingredients in an airtight container.
2. When ready to make breakfast, take a ⅓ cup of the dry mixture and add it to a saucepan with 1 ¼ cup water or milk.
3. Bring the mixture to a boil, before lowering it to a simmer and cooking for 12–15 minutes until thick. Stir occasionally.
4. Remove from heat, add a lid, and allow the mixture to stand for 5 minutes.
5. Add preferred sweetener or topping before serving.

CHAPTER 4

LUNCH AND DINNER RECIPES

Breakfast is meant to get you through the first few hours of the day, but what about afterward? Breakfast may be important, but it isn't the only time to have healthy meals. What if lunch and dinner could be as tantalizing and just as healthy?

POULTRY AND MEATS

Not all meat and poultry are equal. Ideally, you want to only purchase and use lean meats. However, it's the fat that carries most of the flavor, so be sure if you're cooking with slightly fattier meat than normal, trim away excess fat, but keep some handy to help retain flavor.

When choosing meat at the butcher or grocery store, many phrases can make your choice more complicated. Most of the meat sold is from animals that are grain-reared and grain-finished. These animals are raised in small areas and often have more antibiotics than normal. Meat from these animals can affect your gut microbiome.

To prevent this, many people are turning to meat labeled as "grass-fed." However, the term grass-fed can be misleading, as it can be used to describe any animal that spent some time eating grass and is still grain-finished. Unless you can trace the farm the animal was reared on, there is no real way to know if it was grass-fed and grass-finished, as this type of meat isn't regulated. If you want to avoid the excess antibiotics, it's best to look for meat that is labeled as organic, as that is more heavily regulated.

However, organic meat can be very expensive. To avoid the high cost of meat, consider purchasing lean-cut meats or trimming excess fat away yourself. Other factors you'll need to consider when choosing meat are the following:

- It should never have an odor.
- Its color should be a healthy red for red meat and a pale pink to white for poultry.
- It should have a good texture and not feel slimy.
- The butchery or shop should comply with your country's health standards and be clean and odorless.

If you're able to trace where the meat came from, you'll also be able to get a better idea of the quality of life the animals have before arriving on your plate.

HONEY MUSTARD PORK WITH WHITE BEAN MASH AND SPINACH (EF, GF, NF, DF)

When cooked correctly, pork is not only safe but juicy and, with this recipe, only slightly sweet. Pork is high in protein, minerals (zinc, selenium, iron, and phosphorus), as well as vitamins B3, B6, and B12. With a side of mashed beans and spinach, this recipe gives you many anti-inflammatory benefits.

Total Time: 30 minutes
Serving Size: 4
Prep Time: 10 minutes
Cook Time: 20 minutes
Nutritional Facts:
per serving
Calories: 499 kcal
Carbs: 44 g
Fat: 17 g
Protein: 43 g

Ingredients:

- ¼ tsp crushed red pepper
- ½ tsp ground pepper
- ½ tsp salt, divided
- ¾ cup low-sodium chicken broth, divided
- 1 lb spinach, chopped
- 1 ¼ lb pork tenderloin, trimmed
- 1 ½ tsp fresh sage, chopped
- 2 tbsp whole-grain mustard
- 2 garlic cloves, minced
- 2 (15 oz) cans of low-sodium cannellini beans, drained and rinsed
- 3 tbsp EVOO, divided
- 3 tbsp manuka honey

Directions:

1.   Preheat the oven to 425 °F.
2.   Season the tenderloin with half the salt and pepper.
3.   In an oven-safe skillet, heat a tablespoon of oil over medium-high heat.
4.   Place the pork in the hot skillet and cook for 3–5 minutes, turning the meat often to brown all sides.
5.   Add the skillet to the oven, and continue to roast the meat for 12–15 minutes or until the internal temperature has reached 145 °F.
6.   While the pork is cooking, cook the spinach with half of the remaining salt and a tablespoon of oil over medium heat until wilted. Stir frequently while cooking, and transfer to a covered bowl to keep warm afterward.
7.   In a pot over medium heat, add the remaining oil, crushed red pepper, garlic, and sage, and cook for 30 seconds to infuse the oil.
8.   Add half a cup of broth with the remaining salt and beans to the pot and mash the mixture until smooth.
9.   Lower the heat and continue to cook for 5 minutes while stirring often. Cover and remove from heat.
10.   Remove the pork from the oven, and allow it to rest for 5 minutes on a clean cutting board. In the skillet, add the mustard, remaining broth, and honey, and bring to a boil over medium-high heat.
11.   Lower the heat to a simmer for 1–2 minutes as you scrape up any baked-on bits, and mix with the honey mixture until it starts to thicken.
12.   Cut the pork and divide equally with the bean mash and spinach, with a drizzle of the honey sauce.

GINGER BEEF STIR-FRY (DF, GF, EF, NF)

Stir-fry is a great opportunity to get all your vegetables and to make your meal as colorful as possible. You control how spicy your dish is by adjusting the chili–garlic sauce or sriracha. Be wary, as hoisin sauce can contain peanuts.

Total Time: 30 minutes
Serving Size: 4
Prep Time: 20 minutes
Cook Time: 10 minutes
Nutritional Facts:
per serving
Calories: 215 kcal
Carbs: 11 g
Fat: 10 g
Protein: 20 g

Ingredients:

- 1 tbsp tamari, divided
- 1 cup red bell pepper, diced
- 1 cup green bell pepper, diced
- 1 tsp plus 1 tbsp vegetable oil, divided
- 1 small yellow onion, sliced thinly
- 1–3 tsp sriracha or chili–garlic sauce
- 1 ½ tsp cornstarch
- 2 tbsp unsalted chicken broth
- 2 tbsp rice vinegar
- 3 slices peeled ginger, smashed
- 4 tsp unsweetened ketchup
- 4 tsp hoisin sauce
- 12 oz lean flank steak (or chicken breasts), trimmed and cut into 2-inch strips wide and ¼-inch thick

Directions:

1. Take the beef strips and place them in a bowl with half the tamari, a teaspoon of rice vinegar, and cornstarch, and then stir until well combined.

2. Add a teaspoon of oil to the beef mixture until the meat is lightly coated.

3. In a separate bowl, whisk the remaining rice and tamari, hoisin sauce, chili–garlic sauce, and ketchup and set aside.

4. Heat a large skillet until a drop of water vaporizes within a second. Add the remaining oil, coating the skillet before adding the ginger along the edge. Add the beef mixture in an even layer, and allow it to cook undisturbed for a minute, lightly browning it.

5. Add the onion and cook for 30–60 seconds. Remove the beef and onion mixture, keeping the ginger in the skillet.

6. Place the bell peppers in the skillet and cook on high for a minute.

7. Add the beef and onion mixture back to the skillet, plus any liquid that may have accumulated.

8. Pour over the rice vinegar mixture and stir until the beef strips are cooked through, roughly 30–60 seconds. Ginger can be removed if so desired.

LAMB AND BEEF BALTI (GF, EF, NF)

Balti is a type of stew named after the pot it is cooked in. Luckily, you only need a skillet for this recipe. The creamy yogurt source only enhances the turmeric, which gives a beautiful color to the recipe and has many anti-inflammatory properties. If sensitive to beef, double the ground lamb.

Total Time: 1 hour 20 minutes

Serving Size: 4

Prep Time: 10 minutes

Cook Time: 30 minutes (for the stew) plus 40 minutes (for the rice)

Nutritional Facts: per serving

Calories: 531 kcal

Carbs: 58 g

Fat: 20 g

Protein: 31 g

Ingredients:

- ¼ cup low-fat plain Greek yogurt
- ¾ tsp salt
- 1 cup brown basmati rice
- 1 tsp ground cumin
- 1 tbsp ground turmeric
- 1 ½ cups water
- 1 ½ tsp ground coriander
- 2 tbsp Worcestershire sauce
- 2 tbsp garlic, chopped
- 2 tsp fresh ginger, grated
- 3 cups yellow onions, chopped
- 3 cups unsalted beef broth
- 3 tbsp fresh cilantro, chopped
- 3 tbsp tomato paste
- 8 oz ground lamb
- 8 oz lean ground beef

Directions:

1. In a saucepan, add the water and rice and bring to a boil, then lower to a simmer. Cover and continue to cook for 40 minutes or until all water is absorbed.

2. During this time, place the beef and lamb in a large skillet, and cook the meat on medium-high for 5–6 minutes until crumbly and no more pink is visible.

3. Add the onions and continue to cook for 6–8 minutes, until translucent.

4. Raise the temperature, add the herbs and spices, and cook for another minute.

5. Stir in the tomato paste, and cook for a minute before adding the Worcestershire sauce and salt. Stir the mixture while bringing it to a boil.

6. Lower the heat to a simmer and allow the mixture to thicken over 13–15 minutes.

7. Serve the balti over rice and then top with cilantro and yogurt.

TURMERIC CHICKEN (GF, EF, NF, DF)

Turmeric chicken oozes fall goodness with its flavor and beautiful color. Serve with some grains to allow them to soak up the tangy goodness. This meal can last up to four days in the fridge. However, be sure that you store it in glassware, as turmeric stains plastic.

Total Time: 1 hour (with additional 1–2 hours if you want to marinate the chicken)

Serving Size: 6

Prep Time: 5 minutes

Cook Time: 45 minutes

Nutritional Facts:
per serving

Calories: 292 kcal

Carbs: 26 g

Fat: 20 g

Protein: 3 g

Ingredients:

- ½ cup dry white wine or chicken stock
- ½ cup EVOO
- ½ cup fresh orange juice
- 1 large sweet onion, cut into half-moons
- 1 tsp sweet paprika
- 1 lime, juiced
- 1 tsp ground coriander
- 1 large fennel bulb, cored and sliced
- 1 ½ tsp ground turmeric
- 2 medium oranges, unpeeled and sliced
- 2 tbsp yellow mustard
- 2 tsp garlic powder
- 3 tbsp coconut sugar, more for later
- 6 pieces of bone-in, skin-on chicken (chicken legs or breasts or a combination)
- salt and black pepper, to taste
- 1 lime, sliced thinly (optional)

Directions:

1. If not marinating the chicken, preheat the oven to 475 °F.
2. In a large bowl, whisk the wine, orange juice, olive oil, mustard, sugar, and lime juice to make the marinade.
3. In a smaller bowl, add the pepper, turmeric, salt, garlic powder, paprika, and coriander, and mix. Take half of this mixture and add it to the marinade before mixing well.
4. Place the chicken on a clean surface, and pat dry before adding some spices under the skin with most over the top.
5. Add the chicken and remaining ingredients to the bowl of marinade and coat the chicken well.
6. As an optional step, you can allow the chicken to marinate for 1–2 hours, covered in the fridge.
7. Preheat the oven to 475 °F when ready to cook the chicken.
8. Pour the marinade and chicken into a large baking pan and even out the mixture, ensuring the chicken is in a skin-side up position.
9. Bake the chicken for 40–45 minutes, ensuring the skin is brown and the internal temperature is 165–170 °F.
10. Serve with your choice of side.

The Science-Backed Anti-Inflammatory Diet for Beginners

FISH AND SEAFOOD

Any food coming from the ocean is full of omega-3 fatty acids, vitamins B2 (riboflavin) and D, and the minerals calcium, phosphorus, iron, iodine, zinc, and magnesium. Ideally, you want to have at least two portions of fish or seafood a week.

Consuming fish and seafood (shellfish, seaweed, etc.) helps to lower blood pressure, inflammation, and risks of developing serious diseases such as diabetes, arthritis, dementia, and Alzheimer's. It also helps to boost brain function and fight back against depression and attention deficit hyperactivity disorder (ADHD), protects eyes from age-related diseases, and even helps improve sleep quality.

However, pregnant women need to choose low-mercury fish (salmon, trout, and sardines) to prevent the mercury from affecting the developing fetus but still allow the necessary benefits that fish can provide.

GINGER–TAHINI SALMON BAKE (EF, DF, GF, NF)

This salmon bake is rich in color, texture, and taste. From the crunchy green beans to the delicate flavor of the tahini, this sheet-pan dinner is delicious and easy to clean up.

Total Time: 1 hour
Serving Size: 4
Prep Time: 25 minutes
Cook Time: 35 minutes
Nutritional Facts:
per serving
Calories: 555 kcal
Carbs: 37 g
Fat: 30 g
Protein: 38 g

Ingredients:

- ½ tsp salt, divided
- 1 tbsp plus 1 tsp manuka honey
- 1 large sweet potato (roughly 12 oz), cubed
- 1 tbsp plus 2 tsp tahini
- 1 lb white button mushrooms, cut into 1-inch pieces
- 1 lb green beans, trimmed
- 1 ¼ lb salmon, cut into 4 portions
- 1 ½ tsp fresh ginger, grated finely
- 2 tbsp EVOO, divided
- 2 tsp rice vinegar
- 2 tbsp tamari sauce
- 2 tbsp chopped fresh chives (optional)

Directions:

1. Preheat the oven to 425 °F, ensuring the rack is placed 6 inches from the broiler and another below it.
2. In a large bowl, add a tablespoon of oil, ¼ teaspoon salt, mushrooms, and sweet potatoes, and toss until everything is well coated.
3. Spread the vegetable mixture into an even layer on a large, rimmed baking sheet. Place in the oven and bake for 20 minutes, stirring once.
4. During this time, in a separate container, add the remaining salt and oil with the green beans, and toss. Set aside.
5. In a small container, whisk the ginger, tahini, tamari, and honey until well incorporated.
6. Remove the vegetables from the oven. Move the vegetables aside and add the green beans before placing the salmon on top of the vegetables.
7. Pour half the tahini sauce over the salmon, and return the baking sheet to the oven to bake for a further 8–10 minutes, long enough for the fish to flake.
8. Glaze the salmon by turning the broiler on high for 3 minutes on the upper rack.
9. To the remaining tahini sauce, add the vinegar, and drizzle it over the fish and vegetable mixture before serving.

BEET AND SHRIMP WINTER SALAD (EF, NF, DF, GF)

If you're allergic to shellfish, you may want to give this recipe a skip. If not, great! Shrimp is low in calories while high in protein, containing minerals zinc, iodine, copper, phosphorus, magnesium, choline, and selenium, together with vitamins E, B6, and B12. They are also high in omega-3 fatty acids.

Total Time: 15 minutes
Serving Size: 1
Prep Time: 15 minutes
Cook Time: no cooking required
Nutritional Facts:
per serving
Calories: 584 kcal
Carbs: 47 g
Fat: 30 g
Protein: 35 g

Ingredients:

For the Salad

- ½ cup cooked barley
- ½ cup fennel, thinly sliced
- ½ cup zucchini ribbons, julienned or spiralized
- 1 cup cooked beet wedges
- 1 cup lightly packed watercress
- 2 cups lightly packed arugula
- 4 oz cooked, peeled shrimp, tails retained if desired
- fennel fronds, to garnish

For the Vinaigrette

- ⅛ tsp salt
- ¼ tsp ground pepper
- ½ tsp shallot, minced
- ½ tsp Dijon mustard
- 1 tbsp red or white wine vinegar
- 2 tbsp EVOO

Directions:

1. In a large bowl, layer the watercress, arugula, zucchini, beets, barley, fennel, and shrimp.
2. In a smaller bowl, whisk the vinaigrette ingredients before drizzling over the salad.
3. Optionally, garnish with fennel fronds.

TUNISIAN SALAD (NF, DF, GF)

Salads don't have to remain sides; they can be a whole meal. The Tunisian salad is nutritious, satisfying, and bursting with flavors from an array of Mediterranean vegetables. Together with the sweet and savory dressing and a touch of mint, this meal is as great for your gut microbiome as it is for you.

Total Time: 20 minutes
Serving Size:
4 (6 if entrée)
Prep Time: 20 minutes
Cook Time: no cooking required
Nutritional Facts:
per entrée serving
Calories: 299 kcal
Carbs: 16 g
Fat: 20 g
Protein: 16 g

Ingredients:

For the Dressing

- ½–1 lemon, juiced
- ¾ tsp freshly ground black pepper
- ¾ tsp salt
- 1 tbsp flat-leaf parsley, chopped finely
- 1 ½ tbsp white wine vinegar
- 4 tbsp EVOO

For the Salad

- ½ lemon, juiced
- ½ cup whole green olives
- ½ cup whole black olives
- ½–1 red onion, diced finely
- 1 Granny Smith apple, peeled and diced finely
- 1 (5 oz) can oil-packed tuna, drained and flaked
- 1 big handful of fresh mint leaves, chopped finely (or 1 tbsp of dried mint)
- 2 English cucumbers, seeded and diced finely
- 3 green bell peppers, diced finely
- 5 hard-boiled eggs, quartered
- 8 Roma tomatoes, seeded and diced finely
- crusty baguette, for serving (optional)

Directions:

1. Start with the dressing by whisking the lemon juice, oil, salt, vinegar, pepper, and parsley until emulsified. Add more lemon juice to taste.

2. Take the time to carefully clean, seed, and dice the vegetables and add them to a large bowl. Scatter in the mint leaves before drizzling the salad dressing over everything.

3. Scatter the hard-boiled eggs, tuna, and olives over the top of the salad.

4. Enjoy the salad as is, or use crusty baguette slices as a fork for extra fiber.

BAKED BRANZINO (NF, DF, GF, EF)

Otherwise known as the Greek sea bass, the branzino is a mild, almost sweet fish that takes on the flavor of whatever you stuff into it. If you want the fish to take on more of a zesty flavor from the lemons and rosemary, allow it to rest in the fridge for an hour after stuffing it.

Total Time: 40 minutes
Serving Size: 4
Prep Time: 15 minutes
Cook Time: 25 minutes
Nutritional Facts:
per serving
Calories: 380 kcal

Carbs: 7 g

Fat: 13 g

Protein: 53 g

Ingredients:

- ¼ cup flat-leaf parsley, chopped
- ¼ cup lemon juice
- ½ cup white wine (or low-sodium chicken broth)
- 1 red onion, chopped
- 1 tbsp fresh oregano leaves
- 2 tbsp EVOO, divided

- 2 whole branzino fish, cleaned
- 2 sprigs fresh rosemary
- 4 lemon wedges, divided
- salt and ground black pepper, to taste

Directions:

1. Preheat the oven to 325 °F.
2. In a large baking pan, pour in a tablespoon of olive oil with red onion, salt, and pepper to taste, then mix well.
3. Slit each fish lengthwise and place a wedge of lemon, some onions from the baking pan, and a sprig of rosemary inside it before adding it to the pan with the remaining onions. Then carefully fold the fish closed to secure the stuffing before baking.
4. Pour the lemon juice and wine over the mixture and dust with oregano then add a tablespoon of oil over the fish.
5. Place the baking pan in the oven and bake for 25 minutes or until the fish is opaque and flakes with a fork.
6. Use a spatula to remove the bones before serving the fish with lemon wedges and parsley as garnish.

VEGETARIAN MAINS

You don't have to be vegetarian or vegan to enjoy a plant-based meal. Vegetarian meals are all about enjoying more plant-based foods. There are many advantages to including these meals in your diet. Not only does it help lower your environmental footprint, but it's also a healthy choice because of the extra vitamins, phytochemicals, antioxidants, and fiber. Eating less meat helps lower the amount of saturated fat you're consuming, which is one of the causes of inflammation. Whether you're eating more plant-based meals because you want to ensure animal welfare or improving your health, there are many meals you can enjoy!

HEARTY CHILI (GF, V, VG, DF, EF, NF)

Chili isn't just about spice. It's about warmth, comfort, and taste. With the heat from the jalapeños and the robustness of the beans, this chili is filling by itself or with a side of some corn bread.

Total Time: 50 minutes
Serving Size: 6
Prep Time: 10 minutes
Cook Time: 40 minutes
Nutritional Facts:
per serving
Calories: 359 kcal
Carbs: 59 g
Fat: 7 g
Protein: 19 g

Ingredients:

- ¼ tsp black pepper
- ⅓ cup jalapeño peppers, seeded and roughly chopped
- ½ tsp smoked paprika
- 1 yellow onion, diced
- 1 red bell pepper, cored and diced

- 1 tbsp ground cumin
- 1 large carrot, diced
- 1 cup vegetable broth
- 1 (15 oz) can of pinto beans, drained and rinsed
- 1 ½ tsp salt
- 2 tbsp EVOO
- 2 tbsp chili powder
- 2 (15 oz) cans of black beans, drained and rinsed
- 3 garlic cloves, minced
- 8 oz baby bella mushrooms, chopped finely
- 28 oz fire-roasted cherry tomatoes

Directions:

1. Pour the oil into a large pot and heat over medium-high.
2. Add the mushrooms and cook for 5 minutes, stirring now and again.
3. Once the mushrooms are ready, add the bell pepper, carrots, and onions, and cook for 5 minutes before adding the garlic. Cook for an additional 2 minutes.
4. Add the remaining ingredients and stir until well combined. Allow the mixture to simmer over low heat for 30 minutes while stirring occasionally.
5. Ladle the completed chili into a bowl and add any desired toppings.

GOAT CHEESE SANDWICH WITH ARUGULA AND PICKLED BEETS (V, EF, DF)

Not all sandwiches are created equally, and this is proved by the sweet and tangy goat cheese sandwich. Enjoy it as a full meal or a snack, and don't forget the walnuts, as they bring a nutty crunch to the whole mixture. Don't like arugula? Switch it with baby spinach instead.

Total Time: 5 minutes

Serving Size: 1

Prep Time: 5 minutes

Cook Time: no cooking required

Nutritional Facts:
per recipe

Calories: 414 kcal

Carbs: 32 g

Fat: 24 g

Protein: 18 g

The Science-Backed Anti-Inflammatory Diet for Beginners

Ingredients:

- 1 tbsp fresh dill, chopped
- 1 cup arugula
- 1 tbsp chives, snipped
- 1 tbsp walnuts, chopped and toasted
- 1 tsp EVOO
- 2 slices whole wheat sandwich bread, lightly toasted
- 2 oz goat cheese, softened
- 2 oz pickled beets, sliced
- ground pepper, to taste
- a pinch of salt

Directions:

1. In a small bowl, add the cheese, salt, chives, pepper, oil, and dill, and mash until well combined.
2. Spread the mixture on the freshly toasted bread. On one slice, add the walnuts, beets, and arugula before topping with the second slice.
3. Cut to your preferred size before serving.

CHICKPEA AND QUINOA BOWL (V, GF, EF, NF)

The combination of chickpeas and quinoa allows for a meal that isn't only packed with fiber but also full of protein! Better yet? If you have leftover quinoa, it's perfect for the recipe! Even the pepper sauce can be made a few days in advance when added to the fridge.

Total Time: 20 minutes

Serving Size: 4

Prep Time: 20 minutes

Cook Time: no cooking required

Nutritional Facts: per serving

Calories: 479 kcal

Carbs: 50 g

Fat: 25 g

Protein: 13 g

Ingredients:

- ¼ cup red onion, chopped finely
- ¼ cup feta cheese, crumbled
- ¼ cup slivered almonds
- ¼ cup Kalamata olives, chopped
- ½ tsp ground cumin
- 1 (15 oz) can of chickpeas, rinsed
- 1 (7 oz) jar of roasted red peppers, rinsed
- 1 small garlic clove, minced
- 1 cup cucumber, diced
- 1 tsp paprika
- 2 tbsp fresh parsley, chopped finely
- 2 cups cooked quinoa
- 4 tbsp EVOO, divided
- ¼ tsp crushed red pepper (optional)

Directions:

1. In a food processor, add 2 tablespoons of oil, peppers, crushed red pepper, paprika, garlic, almonds, and cumin, and blend until smooth.
2. In a bowl, add the remaining oil, olives, quinoa, and red onion, and mix until well combined.
3. Serve by dividing the quinoa mixture, topped with the pepper sauce, cucumber, and chickpeas, with a sprinkle of parsley and feta.

CHICKPEA PASTA WITH MUSHROOM AND KALE (NF, V, VG, GF, DF, EG)

If you're looking for an alternative to gluten-free pasta, try having chickpea pasta. This has a subtle flavor that will require a little more spicing, which makes it perfect to go with the subtle flavor of the mushrooms, enhanced with the earthiness of the kale.

Total Time: 22 minutes
Serving Size: 4
Prep Time: 5 minutes
Cook Time: 17 minutes
Nutritional Facts:
per serving
Calories: 340 kcal
Carbs: 38 g
Fat: 18 g
Protein: 17 g

Ingredients:

- ¼ cup EVOO
- ½ tsp salt
- ½ tsp dried thyme
- 2 large garlic cloves, sliced
- 8 oz cremini mushrooms, quartered
- 8 oz chickpea rotini or penne
- 8 cups chopped kale
- a pinch of crushed red pepper
- grated Parmesan cheese, for serving (optional)

Directions:

1. Cook the pasta according to the box's instructions (8–10 minutes). Retain a cup of the cooking water when draining.
2. As the pasta cooks, in a large skillet, heat the oil over medium heat before adding the garlic and red pepper. Cook for a minute, then add the salt, thyme, kale, and mushrooms for 5 minutes, stirring occasionally.
3. Once the vegetables are soft, add the pasta, with just enough reserved pasta water to coat it.
4. Cook the mixture for another minute, stirring to ensure everything is well combined.

Regardless of using these recipes for lunch or dinner, as long as you're enjoying a combination of them, you'll be getting a healthy increase of antioxidants. With more antioxidants, you're fighting back against inflammation and improving your health.

Talking about improving your health, many people believe that cutting snacks and desserts from your diet is the best way to be healthy. However, what if those snacks and desserts could contribute to your health? Let's dive into the next chapter to see what extras, sides, and treats you can enjoy healthily.

CHAPTER 5:

SIDES AND EXTRAS

While a meal is meant to be filling, it can further be enhanced by combining it with various sides or extras. Don't be afraid to add your favorite sauces, salads, and desserts to complete a meal. Here are just a few inflammation-fighting extras you can add to your daily routine.

SAUCES, CONDIMENTS, AND DRESSINGS

What are hotdogs without ketchup or salad without Greek dressing? Plain and boring! While store-bought sauces, condiments, and dressing may be tasty, they have ingredients in them that can trigger inflammation. Common ingredients that could trigger inflammation include added sweeteners (artificial or natural), refined oils, trans fats, sodium nitrate, and monosodium glutamate (MSG). These ingredients are often added to improve the shelf life of the product, as well as enhancing taste and color. To avoid these ingredients—and avoid allergens—it's best to make your own food enhancers.

CREAMY AVOCADO GREEK YOGURT DRESSING (V, DF, EF, NF)

Salads are a great way to increase your vegetable intake, yet many people find salads bland. A drizzle of this creamy salad dressing will have you looking at salads in a whole new light.

Total Time: 5 minutes
Serving Size: 8
Prep Time: 5 minutes
Cook Time: no cooking required
Nutritional Facts:
per recipe
Calories: 135 kcal
Carbs: 8 g
Fat: 6 g
Protein: 12 g

Ingredients:

- ¼ cup water
- ½ cup low-fat Greek yogurt
- ½ cup cilantro
- 1 avocado
- 1 garlic clove
- 1 lime, zested and juiced
- sea salt and black pepper, to taste

Directions:

1. Add all the ingredients to a food processor and blend until smooth.
2. To get to the desired consistency, add extra water a teaspoon at a time.
3. Do a taste test and adjust.

 The Science-Backed Anti-Inflammatory Diet for Beginners

HOMEMADE MAYONNAISE (V, DF, GF, NF)

This homemade mayonnaise is all-purpose and can be enjoyed in sandwiches or mixed into chicken or potato salad. Ensure that it's kept in the fridge and used within two weeks.

Total Time: 10 minutes
Serving Size: 1 cup
Prep Time: 10 minutes
Cook Time: no cooking required
Nutritional Facts:
per recipe
Calories: 1,924 kcal
Carbs: 2 g
Fat: 219 g
Protein: 6 g

Ingredients:

- ½ cup EVOO
- ½ cup grape-seed oil
- 1 tbsp fresh lemon juice
- 1 tbsp freshly boiled water
- 1 tsp Dijon mustard
- 2 large egg yolks, room temperature
- salt, to taste

Directions:

1. Mix the olive and grape-seed oil in a cup with a spout for easy pouring.

2. Add all other ingredients, except the boiled water, to a food processor and start blending. While blending, slowly add a few drops of the combined oil, allowing the mixture to thicken and turn a pale yellow.

3. Once the change occurs, increase the rate of pouring while blending to make the mayonnaise creamier.

4. If it's too thick, add some of the boiled water to thin it.

5. Do a taste test and adjust the salt and lemon to your liking before refrigerating.

HOMEMADE KETCHUP (VG, V, DF, GF, EF, NF)

Ketchup is a staple in most homes, but store-bought varieties are high in sugar and other preservatives. Make your own and enjoy having a low-sugar ketchup that will last for two weeks in the fridge.

Total Time: 55 minutes
Serving Size: 2 cups
Prep Time: 10 minutes
Cook Time: 45 minutes
Nutritional Facts:
per recipe
Calories: 1,055 kcal
Carbs: 225 g
Fat: 18 g
Protein: 17 g

Ingredients:

- ½ tsp ground coriander
- ½ tsp chili powder
- ½ tsp ground cumin
- ½ cup apple cider vinegar
- ½ tsp ground ginger
- 1 cup coconut palm sugar (or stevia, to taste)
- 1 small onion, minced
- 1 tbsp EVOO
- 1 large garlic clove, minced
- 4 lb ripe tomatoes
- a pinch of nutmeg
- a pinch of ground cinnamon
- cayenne pepper, to taste
- salt, to taste

Directions:

1. In a large saucepan, bring water to a boil while filling a large bowl with ice water.

2. Cut a shallow X at the bottom of each tomato and place them in the boiling water for 15–20 seconds before adding to the ice water. Leave them there for 2–3 minutes.

3. Remove the tomatoes and pull the skins free before cutting the fruit crosswise.

The Science-Backed Anti-Inflammatory Diet for Beginners

4. Place a strainer over a bowl, and remove the seeds of the tomatoes, pressing on them to release all their juices. Throw away the seeds, then finely chop the tomatoes and add them to the juice strained.

5. Drain the large saucepan and heat the oil over medium heat.

6. Add the garlic and onions and cook for 4 minutes before adding the nutmeg, coriander, cumin, cinnamon, ginger, and chili powder, and cook for 30 seconds.

7. Pour in the vinegar and tomatoes, and continue to cook over medium heat for 30 minutes while stirring occasionally. The liquid should be reduced, and the tomatoes no longer solid.

8. Add half the sugar and lower the temperature to low, continuing to stir and cook for a further 10–15 minutes, allowing the mixture to thicken.

9. Do a taste test and decide if you want a sweeter ketchup before adding the remaining sugar.

10. Further season with cayenne and salt, remove from the heat, and allow it to cool.

11. Pour the liquid into an airtight container and place it in the fridge.

VEGAN SOUR CREAM (VG, V, DF, GF, EF)

Why buy vegan sour cream when it's so easy to make yourself beforehand? This creamy condiment is perfect for those cut veggies at snack time or as a topping on a taco. Use this within a week.

Total Time: 15 minutes

Serving Size: 12

Prep Time: 5 minutes

Cook Time: no cooking required

Nutritional Facts: per serving

Calories: 18 kcal

Carbs: 1 g

Fat: 1.4 g

Protein: 0.5 g

Ingredients:

- ¼ cup lemon juice
- ¼ cup cashews, soaked for 1–2 hours beforehand
- ¼ tsp salt
- ⅓ cup water
- ⅔ cup ice

Directions:

1. After soaking the cashews, add all the ingredients to a blender, and process until smooth.

SALADS, SOUPS, AND STEWS

There is nothing quite as adaptable and versatile as stews, soups, and salads. While many can be made from scratch, it's also easy to make them from any leftovers you have in your fridge. Enjoy it according to your unique needs, regardless of the time of year and season.

EASY RATATOUILLE (VG, V, DF, GF, EF, NF)

Ratatouille is a classic, summer vegetable stew full of soft-cooked vegetables and homey spices. Enjoy it as is or topped with an egg or two to make a full meal.

Total Time: 55 minutes

Serving Size: 6

Prep Time: 20 minutes

Cook Time: 35 minutes

Nutritional Facts:
per serving

Calories: 97 kcal

Carbs: 18 g

Fat: 0.8 g

Protein: 3.7 g

Ingredients:

- ½ cup red wine (or low-sodium beef stock)
- 1 tsp dried rosemary
- 1 lb eggplant, peeled and cut into inch pieces
- 1 tsp black pepper
- 1 tbsp sherry vinegar or lime juice
- 1 yellow onion, finely chopped
- 1 tsp sweet paprika
- 2 zucchinis, sliced into ½-inch half-moons
- 2 bell peppers (mixture of colors), sliced into inch pieces
- 2 sprigs fresh thyme
- 2 lb tomatoes, chopped
- 3 tbsp fresh basil, chopped
- 6 garlic cloves, minced
- kosher salt
- EVOO

To Serve

- crusty, gluten-free bread
- sunny-side up eggs

Directions:

1. Start by salting the eggplant to get rid of the bitterness. Sprinkle salt over the pieces and mix, allowing it to stand for 20 minutes. Afterward, remove excess salt and liquid by patting dry with a paper towel.
2. In a large pot, add the olive oil and heat over medium heat. Once simmering, add in the onions and cook for 5 minutes.
3. Add the bell peppers and cook for 4 minutes, stirring now and again.
4. To the mixture, add the remaining ingredients, except the sherry vinegar and basil, and season with salt to taste.
5. Increase the temperature to medium-high and boil the mixture for 5 minutes, stirring infrequently. Lower

the temperature to bring the mixture to a simmer on low before covering and allowing it to cook for another 20 minutes.

6. Remove the pot from the heat, and pour in the sherry vinegar and some olive oil before topping with basil.

7. Ratatouille can rest for an hour before serving or can be served immediately. Top with any optional ingredient.

GREEK SALAD WITH EDAMAME (NF, EF, GF, V)

The classic Greek salad may be fine as it is, but with the addition of edamame, you're creating a delicious, high-protein salad.

Total Time: 20 minutes
Serving Size: 4
Prep Time: 20 minutes
Cook Time: no cooking required
Nutritional Facts:
per serving
Calories: 344 kcal
Carbs: 20 g
Fat: 23 g
Protein: 17 g

Ingredients:

- ¼ tsp ground pepper
- ¼ cup red onion, slivered
- ¼ cup red wine vinegar
- ¼ tsp salt
- ¼ cup Kalamata olives, sliced
- ¼ cup fresh basil, slivered
- ½ cup feta cheese, crumbled
- ½ cucumber, sliced
- 1 cup cherry or grape tomatoes, halved
- 3 tbsp EVOO
- 8 cups romaine lettuce, chopped roughly
- 16 oz (about 3 cups) frozen edamame, shelled and thawed

Directions:

1. In a large bowl, mix the pepper, vinegar, salt, and oil until combined.
2. Add the remaining ingredients and toss to coat.

QUINOA MEDITERRANEAN SALAD (NF, EF, GF, V)

Mediterranean salads are heralded as being the pinnacle of healthy salads. The only way it can improve is with the nutty, fiber-filled addition of quinoa.

Total Time: 45 minutes
Serving Size: 6
Prep Time: 15 minutes
Cook Time: no cooking, only 30-minute resting period
Nutritional Facts: per serving
Calories: 472 kcal
Carbs: 39 g
Fat: 30 g
Protein: 12 g

Ingredients:

- ¼ tsp crushed red pepper
- ½ cup EVOO
- ½ cup Kalamata olives, pitted and halved
- 1 cup crumbled feta, divided
- 1 cup grape tomatoes, halved
- 1 (15 oz) can of salt-free chickpeas, rinsed
- 1 ½ tsp manuka honey
- 1 ½ cups red onion, thinly sliced
- 1 ½ tsp Dijon mustard
- 2 cups cucumber, sliced thinly
- 3 cups (about 3 oz) baby spinach
- 3 tbsp fresh oregano, chopped
- 3 cups cooked quinoa, fully cooled
- 6 tbsp red wine vinegar

Directions:

1. In a large bowl, whisk the crushed red pepper, oil, Dijon, vinegar, honey, and oregano until combined.
2. Add half the feta with the quinoa, chickpeas, cucumber, olives, tomatoes, and onions, and toss until coated.
3. Cover the salad and allow it to rest for 30 minutes in the fridge.
4. After resting, add the spinach and toss once more before adding the remaining feta, and serve.

CREAMY KALE AND BRUSSEL'S SPROUT SALAD (V, VG, DF, GF, EF, NF)

Another twist on the classic Caesar salad, but instead of lettuce, dark green vegetables are used, boosting your vitamin A and K intake.

Total Time: 15 minutes
Serving Size: 6
Prep Time: 10 minutes
Cook Time: 5 minutes
Nutritional Facts:
per serving
Calories: 237 kcal
Carbs: 21 g
Fat: 16 g
Protein: 7 g

Ingredients:

- ¼ tsp salt
- ¼ cup EVOO
- ¼ cup whole wheat or gluten-free panko bread crumbs
- 1 tbsp unsalted butter
- 1 tsp ground pepper
- 1 tbsp white miso or tahini sauce
- 1 (6 oz) small avocado, mashed
- 1 tsp Dijon mustard
- 2 garlic cloves, grated
- 2 (16 oz) kale bunches,

stemmed and chopped

- 2 garlic cloves, grated
- 2 tbsp grated Parmesan or vegan cheese
- 3 tbsp fresh lemon juice
- 12 oz fresh Brussels sprouts, trimmed and thinly sliced

Directions:

1. Over medium heat, add the butter to a skillet and cook for 2–3 minutes, allowing it to become golden and get a nutty smell.
2. Pour in the panko crumbs and stir as they become coated in butter. Cook for 1–2 minutes and then place on a paper towel-lined bowl.
3. Add the salt, avocado, pepper, lemon juice, garlic, miso, and Parmesan cheese to a blender and process for 30 seconds or until smooth. Pour in the oil and blend for another 30–60 seconds. Transfer to a large bowl.
4. Add the kale to the bowl, and massage the leaves into the dressing for 1–2 minutes, helping to soften the leaves.
5. Slice the Brussels sprouts to the preferred thickness, and add to the salad before tossing.
6. Scatter the bread crumbs over and serve.

CHICKEN STOCK (DF, GF, EF, NF)

Making chicken stock is as easy as retaining the chicken carcass once you've taken the meat for other uses. This is a great alternative to buying chicken stock as it's practically salt-free and you're recycling food you'd normally throw away. The stock can last five days in the fridge but up to six months in the freezer.

Total Time: 3 hours 10 minutes

Serving Size: 6

Prep Time: 10 minutes

Cook Time: 3 hours

Nutritional Facts: per serving

Calories: 19 kcal

Carbs: 4.5 g

Fat: 0.1 g

Protein: 0.6 g

Ingredients:

- 1 chicken carcass
- 1 onion, quartered
- 2 celery ribs, chopped
- 2 bay leaves
- 2 large carrots, chopped
- 3 garlic cloves, crushed
- 4 sprigs fresh thyme
- parsley stems
- 10 peppercorns (optional)

Directions:

1. Strip as much meat from the chicken carcass as possible, to use in other recipes.
2. Place the carcass, other bones, and skin (optional) in a Dutch oven or large stockpot. Add the remaining ingredients.
3. Place the stockpot over medium heat, and pour in 10 cups of cold water before bringing the mixture to a low boil.
4. Lower the temperature to bring the mixture to a simmer. Don't keep it to a boil, as this will result in the protein and fat emulsifying and produce a greasy stock.
5. Keep the mixture at a simmer for 3 hours, skimming the surface every 45 minutes of any foam (scum) that forms.
6. Over a large bowl, place a mesh strainer lined with cheesecloth.
7. Ladle the stock over the strainer until all the liquid has passed through. Press down on any solids collected to release more liquid.
8. Allow the stock to cool to room temperature before transferring to preferred containers and moving to the fridge overnight.
9. Remove any fat on the surface, and retain the jelly-like stock in the fridge or freezer until it is needed.

    The Science-Backed Anti-Inflammatory Diet for Beginners

PEA SOUP (DF, GF, EF, NF)

This lovely spring soup is ideal for homegrown leftover peas or frozen peas. It creates a beautiful green color high in vitamin C and flavor. It can last up to four days in the fridge and three months in the freezer.

Total Time: 30 minutes
Serving Size: 4
Prep Time: 15 minutes
Cook Time: 15 minutes
Nutritional Facts:
per serving
Calories: 287 kcal
Carbs: 38 g
Fat: 9 g
Protein: 17 g

Ingredients:

- ½ cup water
- ½ tsp salt
- 1 tbsp butter
- 1 stalk celery, chopped
- 1 tbsp EVOO
- 1 tsp fresh thyme or parsley, chopped
- 1 medium onion, chopped
- 2 garlic cloves, chopped
- 4 cups low-sodium chicken broth or vegetable broth
- 6 cups peas, fresh or frozen
- freshly ground pepper, to taste
- ½ cup almond milk (optional)

Directions:

1. In a large stockpot, heat the butter over medium heat until it melts.
2. Add the celery and onions and cook for 4–6 minutes until soft.
3. Stir in the thyme (or parsley) and cook for 10 seconds.
4. Pour in the water, broth, and peas, then simmer on high heat.
5. Lower the temperature to prevent the mixture from

boiling, but maintain the simmer, and continue to cook for a minute or until the peas are tender.

6. Purée the mixture in batches until smooth.
7. Stir in the almond milk and season with salt and pepper.

DESSERTS

Unlike most diets that will tell you to give up the sugary treats, the anti-inflammatory diet encourages a sweet treat now and again. Treat yourself to some of the irresistible, tasty desserts that are sure to wrap up any meal. Forcing yourself to avoid these treats could lead to cravings, which can lead to binging and even a binging eating disorder.

LEMON–BLUEBERRY POKE CAKE (V, NF)

The combination of the tangy–sour lemon with the sweetness of the blueberries makes this a cake that everyone will be clamoring to have more of.

Total Time:
1 hour 35 minutes
Serving Size: 10
Prep Time: 35 minutes
Cook Time: 1 hour
Nutritional Facts:
per serving
Calories: 335 kcal
Carbs: 52 g
Fat: 13 g
Protein: 5 g

Ingredients:

- ¼ tsp salt
- ⅓ cup low-fat plain Greek yogurt
- ½ cup EVOO
- ½ tsp baking soda
- ¾ cup gluten-free all-

purpose flour

- 1 tsp vanilla extract
- 1 tsp baking powder
- 1 cup whole wheat pastry flour
- 1 ¼ coconut sugar, divided
- 1 ½ cups fresh blueberries
- 2 tbsp lemon zest
- 2 large eggs
- 5 tbsp lemon juice

Directions:

1. Preheat the oven to 350 °F.
2. Prepare a 9 x 5-inch loaf pan by coating it with cooking spray.
3. In a large bowl, beat the vanilla, ¾ cup sugar, lemon zest, yogurt, and oil with an electric mixer on medium until well combined.
4. Add the eggs to the mixture and beat well.
5. In a medium bowl, whisk the remaining dry ingredients before adding the mixture and the blueberries to the wet mixture. Fold it until just mixed.
6. Pour the batter into the prepared loaf pan and bake for an hour. The cake should be golden, and a toothpick should come out clean when inserted into the center.
7. Let the cake cool in the pan for 5 minutes before running a knife along the edges of the pan. Invert the pan onto a wire rack until the cake comes free. Place the cake back in the pan.
8. In a small bowl, make the glaze by whisking the remaining sugar and lemon juice until the sugar dissolves.
9. Use a skewer to poke multiple 1 ½-inch holes over the top of the cake.
10. Slowly pour the glaze over the top of the cake, allowing it to soak into the holes. Leave the cake to soak for 15 minutes.
11. Remove the cake from the pan and allow it to fully cool before slicing and serving.

YOGURT BARK (V, GF, EF, NF)

Bark is one of those sweet treats that is so versatile it can be used to represent the holidays or the different seasons. Yogurt bark is a healthier alternative to chocolate bark and is great for those hot summer days.

Total Time:
3 hours 10 minutes

Serving Size: 32

Prep Time: 10 minutes plus 3 hours (for freezing)

Cook Time: no cooking required

Nutritional Facts:
per serving

Calories: 34 kcal

Carbs: 4 g

Fat: 1 g

Protein: 2 g

Ingredients:

- ¼ cup maple syrup
- ¼ cup 70% (or more) dark mini chocolate chips (or cocoa nibs)
- 1 tsp vanilla extract
- 1 ½ cups sliced strawberries
- 3 cups Greek yogurt

Directions:

1. Place parchment paper in a large-rimmed baking sheet, ideally a 10 x 15-inch baking sheet.
2. In a medium bowl, combine the vanilla, maple syrup, and yogurt before spreading the mixture on the prepared baking sheet.
3. Scatter the chocolate and strawberries over the top and freeze for at least 3 hours.
4. Once firm, cut or break the bark and serve or return to the freezer.

The Science-Backed Anti-Inflammatory Diet for Beginners

LEMON–BLUEBERRY NICE CREAM
(VG, V, DF, GF, EF, NF)

Who doesn't love ice cream on a hot day? People who are lactose intolerant. Luckily, this refreshing lemon–blueberry nice cream is just the treat you need, without the fear of your body turning on you. Nice cream can last up to a month in the freezer.

Total Time: 10 minutes

Serving Size: 4

Prep Time: 10 minutes

Cook Time: no cooking required

Nutritional Facts:
per serving

Calories: 98 kcal

Carbs: 25 g

Fat: 1 g

Protein: 1 g

Ingredients:

- ¼ tsp vanilla extract
- ¼ cup lemon juice
- ¼ cup cold water, as needed
- ¾ cup frozen blueberries
- 3 medium ripe bananas, sliced and frozen

Directions:

1. Add the vanilla, banana, and lemon juice to a food processor, and blend until smooth. Pour in some water to loosen the mixture if needed, a teaspoon at a time.

2. Pour the mixture into a freezer-safe container with a lid, and stir in the blueberries.

3. Serve immediately or place in the freezer for later use.

APPLE CRISP WITH CRANBERRIES (VG, V, DF, GF, EF, NF)

There is nothing better than a warm apple pie with a side of low-sugar ice or nice cream. With the addition of the cranberries, you'll not only get a sweet treat but a boost to your vitamin C intake.

Total Time:
1 hour 10 minutes

Serving Size: 12

Prep Time: 10 minutes

Cook Time: 40 minutes (for cooking) plus 20 minutes (for cooling)

Nutritional Facts:
per serving

Calories: 302 kcal

Carbs: 40 g

Fat: 17 g

Protein: 3 g

Ingredients:

- ½ cup coconut sugar
- ½ tsp salt
- ½ cup gluten-free flour
- ½ cup EVOO
- ¾ tsp ground cinnamon
- 1 cup nuts, chopped
- 1 cup dried cranberries
- 1 cup rolled oats
- 2 tbsp lemon juice
- 2 tbsp cornstarch or potato starch
- 8 cups apple and pear mixture, diced or sliced

Directions:

1. Preheat the oven to 350 °F.
2. Add all the fruits with the lemon juice and cornstarch in a large bowl.
3. Transfer to a 9 x 13-inch baking dish and spread evenly.

4. In a separate bowl, add the remaining ingredients and mix before pouring over the fruit.

5. Place the baking dish in the oven and bake for 30–40 minutes, ensuring the fruit is tender and the top is brown.

6. Allow to cool for 20 minutes before serving.

One of the most difficult times to start a new diet is during the holiday season. There are so many different foods to try, it's difficult to say no to your old favorites. However, there is no reason to avoid these meals when there are so many different ways to prepare all your favorites without spiking your inflammation. Let's dive into the holiday recipes!

CHAPTER 6

HOLIDAY RECIPES

Don't let holiday blues get you down because you can't celebrate with the people you love. The anti-inflammatory diet doesn't seek to take away from the festivities but rather add to it!

CHRISTMAS DINNER

GINGER SALMON (DF, GF, EF, NF)

Instead of the traditional turkey, opt for a lean protein such as salmon for omega-3 fatty acids with just a hint of ginger to make it Christmassy.

Total Time: 43 minutes
Serving Size: 2
Prep Time: 35 minutes
Cook Time: 8 minutes
Nutritional Facts:
per serving
Calories: 225 kcal
Carbs: 3 g
Fat: 14 g
Protein: 23 g

Ingredients:

- ¼ cup water
- 1 tbsp coconut oil
- 1 tbsp plum vinegar
- 2 tsp fresh ginger, grated
- 2 pieces (4 oz) wild salmon fillets
- lime slices, for garnish

Directions:

1. In a shallow baking dish, combine the vinegar, water, oil, and ginger.
2. Place the fish in the marinade, ensuring it's covered before placing it in the fridge for 30 minutes.
3. Preheat the oven to its low broiler setting.
4. Place the fish in an oven-safe dish skin-side up, and bake in the oven for 6–8 minutes.
5. Baste the fish with the remaining marinade at least twice while in the oven.
6. Serve with lime slices as garnish.

GREEN BEANS ALMONDINE (VG, V, DF, GF, EF)

Sautéed crunchy beans with a hint of garlic, while enhanced with nutty almonds, are the perfect side for any Christmas meal.

Total Time: 12 minutes
Serving Size: 4
Prep Time: 2 minutes
Cook Time: 10 minutes
Nutritional Facts:
per serving
Calories: 139 kcal
Carbs: 10 g
Fat: 11 g
Protein: 4 g

Ingredients:

- ¼ cup slivered almonds
- ½ tsp salt
- ½ tsp pepper
- 1 lb (about 4 cups) green beans, trimmed
- 1 tbsp garlic, minced
- 2 tbsp water
- 2 tbsp EVOO

Directions:

1. In a pan over medium-high, heat the olive oil before adding the garlic, and sauté for a minute.
2. Add the salt, beans, and pepper and sauté for 1–2 minutes.

3. Pour in the water and cover, allowing the beans to steam for 5 minutes on low heat. Stir occasionally.

4. Remove the lid, scatter in the slivered almonds, and continue to sauté for 1–2 minutes, allowing the liquid from the pan to evaporate.

CINNAMON BAKED APPLES (VG, V, DF, GF, EF)

Cinnamon is another scent often associated with Christmas. So while everyone is enjoying the main meal, allow this dessert's scent to permeate your home with the smell of Christmas.

Total Time: 45 minutes
Serving Size: 8
Prep Time: 10 minutes
Cook Time: 35 minutes
Nutritional Facts:
per serving
Calories: 320 kcal
Carbs: 37 g
Fat: 20 g
Protein: 4 g

Ingredients:

- ½ cup almond flour
- 1 tbsp manuka honey
- 1 tsp ground ginger
- 1 cup rolled oats
- 1 cup vegan or coconut butter
- 1 tsp vanilla extract
- 2 tsp cinnamon
- 2 tsp lemon juice
- 5 cups apples, skinned and sliced

Directions:

1. Preheat the oven to 375 °F.

2. In a large bowl, add a teaspoon of cinnamon, the apple slices, lemon juice, vanilla, and ginger, and mix until combined.

3. Pour apple mixture into a 9 x 9-inch baking dish and set aside.

4. In a clean bowl, mix the remaining cinnamon, almond flour, honey, and oats before mixing and pouring over the apple mixture.

5. Cut the butter into pea-sized pieces and scatter it over the top of the mixture. Don't mix!

6. Place the baking tray in the oven and bake for 35 minutes. The dish should be ready once the apple mixture is bubbling and the topping starts to turn golden brown.

CRISPY OVEN-ROASTED POTATOES (VG, V, DF, GF, EF, NF)

No Christmas is perfect without a side of roasted potatoes, and this recipe is far healthier than most.

Total Time: 45 minutes
Serving Size: 6
Prep Time: 5 minutes
Cook Time: 40 minutes
Nutritional Facts:
per serving
Calories: 126 kcal
Carbs: 19 g
Fat: 4 g
Protein: 2 g

Ingredients:

- ½ tsp garlic powder
- ½ tsp salt
- ½ tsp onion powder
- ½ tsp pepper
- 2 tbsp olive oil
- 4 cups Yukon Gold potatoes, cubed into ½-inch pieces

Directions:

1. Preheat the oven to 450 °F and prepare a baking sheet by lining it with parchment paper.

2. Add all the ingredients to a large bowl, and toss until

the potatoes are evenly coated.

3. Place the potatoes in the baking dish, ensuring they are spread out evenly.

4. Bake for 20 minutes before stirring the potatoes to ensure even cooking, and bake for another 20 minutes until golden brown.

HOLIDAY PARTIES

Perhaps you're not cooking this year but have been asked to bring something to a party. Give these party treats a try to wow your friends, family, and colleagues.

HALLOWEEN DIP (VG, V, DF, GF, EF, NF)

Fall is the perfect time to use pumpkins in everything. Combine this vitamin A-strong vegetable with chickpeas to make a delightfully festive Halloween dip.

Total Time: 1 hour
Serving Size: 8
Prep Time: 10 minutes
Cook Time: 50 minutes
Nutritional Facts:
per serving
Calories: 123 kcal
Carbs: 8 g
Fat: 7 g
Protein: 4 g

Ingredients:

- ½ lemon, juiced
- 1 (14 oz) can chickpeas, drained and rinsed
- 1 yellow pepper, seeded and sliced
- 1 (about 1.1 lb) small pumpkin
- 1 red pepper, seeded and sliced
- 2 tbsp tahini paste
- 2 garlic cloves, peeled
- EVOO, for roasting

Directions:

1. Preheat the oven to 400 °F.
2. Cut the pumpkin two thirds of the way up, and remove the top to get rid of the seeds.
3. Cut the pumpkin into manageable pieces and place on a rimmed baking sheet with a generous helping of olive oil and garlic. Season to taste with salt and pepper as needed. Bake for 45 minutes.
4. Allow the pumpkin to cool completely before placing the pieces, everything remaining on the baking sheet, chickpeas, tahini paste, and lemon juice into a blender, and processing until smooth.
5. Do a taste test, and season to taste if required. Extra oil can be added if the mixture is too thick.
6. Serve hummus with the cut vegetables and any optional ingredients.

TURKEY BALLS (DF, GF, NF)

Whether you have leftover turkey you can grind up or have bought ground turkey, this recipe is for you. These bite-sized snacks are perfect for every opportunity, so don't just keep them for Thanksgiving.

Total Time: 55 minutes
Serving Size: 42
Prep Time: 25 minutes
Cook Time: 30 minutes
Nutritional Facts:
per serving
Calories: 46 kcal
Carbs: 7 g
Fat: 1 g
Protein: 2 g

Ingredients:

For the Turkey Balls

- ¼ tsp ground ginger
- ¼ tsp salt
- ¼ tsp ground cinnamon

- ¼ cup onion, chopped finely
- ¼ tsp pepper
- ½ tsp curry powder
- ½ cup dry gluten-free bread crumbs
- 1 large egg, beaten
- 1 lb ground turkey

For the Sauce

- ¼ cup Dijon mustard
- ½ tsp ground ginger
- ½ tsp curry powder
- 1 cup manuka honey

Optional

- fresh mint leaves
- fresh basil leaves
- lime wedges
- fresh cilantro

Directions:

1. Preheat the oven to 350 °F.
2. Grease a 15 x 10-inch baking pan.
3. Add all the turkey ball ingredients together, and mix well before adding the turkey. Shape the mixture into one-inch balls, then place them on the prepared baking pan.
4. Bake for 20–25 minutes until cooked through and juice runs clear.
5. While the balls are cooking, add all the sauce ingredients in a small saucepan, and whisk well over medium heat until the mixture is warmed through.
6. Take ¼ cup of the sauce, and brush it over the balls before returning them to the oven to bake for another 10 minutes.
7. Serve the balls with the remaining sauce and optional fresh herbs and lime wedges. This can be served hot or cold.

STUFFED MUSHROOMS (V, EF, NF)

A classic finger food that can be highly adaptable when it comes to dipping sauces, or you can enjoy it as is with the cheesy goodness.

Total Time: 50 minutes

Serving Size: 10

Prep Time: 20 minutes

Cook Time: 30 minutes

Nutritional Facts: per serving

Calories: 75 kcal

Carbs: 7 g

Fat: 4 g

Protein: 4 g

Ingredients:

- ¼ cup plus 3 tbsp whole wheat panko, divided
- ½ tsp black pepper
- ½ tsp kosher salt
- 1 oz (about ¼ cup) Parmesan cheese, grated
- 1 tbsp olive oil
- 1 tbsp fresh thyme, chopped
- 1 tbsp garlic, chopped
- 1 ½ lb (about 30 mushrooms) medium-sized fresh button mushrooms
- 2 tbsp fresh parsley, chopped
- 4 oz low-fat cream cheese or "cashew" cheese if sensitive to dairy

Directions:

1. Preheat the oven to 400 °F.
2. Prepare a large-rimmed baking sheet by lightly coating it with cooking spray.
3. Thoroughly clean the mushrooms, ensuring there is no dirt, before removing the stems and retaining them.
4. Place the mushroom caps down on the baking sheet.
5. Finely chop the mushroom stems as you heat oil over medium-high heat in a skillet.
6. Add the chopped mushrooms to the skillet with garlic, pepper, and salt, and cook for 6 minutes or until the mushrooms turn golden brown. There shouldn't be much liquid remaining.
7. To the mushroom stems, add ¼ cup of panko and stir for a minute to allow them to turn golden brown. Then add 2 tablespoons of parmesan cheese with the cream cheese, thyme, and parsley, and immediately remove from heat while stirring the mixture until well combined.
8. Spoon in a teaspoon of the cheese mixture into each mushroom cap.
9. In a small bowl, combine the remaining panko and Parmesan cheese before taking each mushroom cap

and dipping it stuffing-side into the mixture to lightly coat.

10. Return mushrooms to the baking sheet and lightly spray with cooking spray before baking in the oven for 20–22 minutes. The stuffing should be golden brown.

ENERGY BALLS (VG, V, DF, GF, EG)

Don't forget to include some tasty sweets for holiday office parties. These little bundles of energy will get everyone through the holidays without feeling too drained. They can last three days in the fridge and up to three months in the freezer.

Total Time: 15 minutes
Serving Size: 20 balls
Prep Time: 15 minutes
Cook Time: no cooking required
Nutritional Facts: per serving
Calories: 70 kcal
Carbs: 10 g
Fat: 3 g
Protein: 2 g

Ingredients:

- ⅓ cup unsweetened shredded coconut
- 1 cup almonds, chopped
- 1 cup dried apricots
- 1 cup dried figs

Directions:

1. Add the dried fruit and almonds to a food processor and pulse until everything is chopped finely.
2. Shape the mixture into balls and roll in coconut.

HANUKKAH CELEBRATION

Hanukkah is an eight-day Jewish holiday that is filled with all manner of tasty treats you can enjoy.

BRISKET AND ROOTS (DF, GF, EF, NF)

Low and slow is the best way to enjoy a juicy and soft brisket, but don't forget the delicious earthy roots to add to your anti-inflammatory diet.

Total Time:
5 hours 40 minutes
Serving Size: 8
Prep Time: 10 minutes
Cook Time:
5 hours and 30 minutes
Nutritional Facts:
per serving
Calories: 275 kcal
Carbs: 19 g
Fat: 6 g
Protein: 27 g

Ingredients:

- ½ tsp freshly ground pepper
- ½ tsp salt
- 1 tbsp EVOO
- 1 medium (about ¾ lb) rutabaga, peeled
- 1 tsp sweet paprika
- 1–2 tbsp water
- 1 tsp Dijon mustard
- 1 cup low-salt chicken stock
- 2 lb flat, first-cut brisket, trimmed, preferably grass-fed
- 2 tsp arrowroot or potato starch
- 2 tsp fresh (or ¾ tsp dried) thyme, chopped
- 2 bay leaves
- 3 medium parsnips, peeled and cored
- 3 medium onions, sliced
- 3 cups low-salt beef broth
- 4 medium carrots, peeled
- a pinch of ground allspice

Directions:

1. Preheat the oven to 325 °F.
2. Add the oil to an oven-safe stockpot and place over medium-high heat.
3. Place the brisket in the pot and cook for 3–5 minutes per side. Remove and place on a large plate.
4. To the same pot, add the onion to cook for 2 minutes while continuing to stir. Once translucent, add the bay leaves, allspice, pepper, thyme, salt, and paprika. Pour in the chicken stock, then bring to a boil for 3 minutes.
5. Return the brisket to the pot, with any juices on the plate. Cover and place the oven-safe stockpot in the oven to bake for 1 ½ hours.
6. While the brisket bakes, prepare the rutabaga, carrots, and parsnips. Cut them into 2 x 2 ½-inch sticks.
7. Remove the brisket from the stockpot and set aside. Remove the bay leaves, and stir the mustard into the stockpot, followed by the root vegetables.
8. Place the brisket back and bake for another hour.
9. Test the meat and vegetables to ensure they're tender before removing them and placing them on a platter, then cover them with tinfoil.
10. If not tender, continue to bake for another 20 minutes and test again. The thickness of the brisket will influence the baking time, and it can be as long as 5 hours.
11. Use a spoon to skim any floating fat from the sauce before adding the pot to the stove on high and bringing it to a boil. Reduce to a simmer for 5 minutes to intensify flavors as you stir.
12. Dissolve the arrowroot in a tablespoon of water before adding it to the simmering pot. Continue to stir as the mixture thickens for the next 10 seconds. Remove from heat.
13. Cut the brisket thinly before serving with a side of cooked vegetables and pouring some of the sauce over.

The Science-Backed Anti-Inflammatory Diet for Beginners

CANDIED SWEET POTATO LATKES (V, DF, GF, NF)

Latkes can be a side or a dessert, depending on your taste. If you're not prepared to enjoy them immediately, freeze them as a single layer for several months.

Total Time: 40 minutes
Serving Size: 10
Prep Time: 15 minutes
Cook Time: 25 minutes
Nutritional Facts:
per serving
Calories: 161 kcal
Carbs: 26 g
Fat: 5 g
Protein: 2 g

Ingredients:

- ¼ tsp ground cinnamon
- ½ tsp vanilla extract
- 1 tsp orange juice or ¼ tsp orange zest
- 1 small sweet onion, chopped finely
- 1 egg white, beaten
- 1 tbsp pure maple syrup
- 1 large egg, beaten
- 2 tbsp coconut palm sugar
- 2 lb sweet potatoes, peeled and shredded
- 2 tbsp EVOO, divided
- 2 tsp kosher salt
- 2 tbsp coconut butter, divided
- 6 tbsp tapioca flour
- a pinch of freshly grated nutmeg

Directions:

1. Add all the ingredients, except the olive oil and butter, to a large bowl and mix well. Allow the mixture to rest for 10 minutes.

2. After resting, transfer the mixture to a mesh strainer, and squeeze the remaining liquid out. Continue to do this until no more liquid can be removed. Excess liquid will make the latkes fall apart.

3. To a large frying pan, add ½ tablespoon of butter and oil to grease the pan placed over medium heat.

4. Take a rounded tablespoon of the sweet potato mixture, flatten it to make the latkes, and add them to the frying pan.

5. Cook for 8 minutes before flipping and cooking for another 5 minutes, allowing them to brown. Don't disturb the latkes while cooking as this may cause them to fall apart.

6. After cooking, add the latkes to a paper towel-lined plate and serve.

7. Latkes can be refrigerated for later use. To warm before serving, preheat the oven to 325 °F, and allow the latkes to bake for 15–20 minutes before serving.

APPLESAUCE (VG, V, DF, GF, EF, NF)

Never use store-bought applesauce ever again. This recipe contains no added sugar and is great to enjoy with some fruits or as a replacement for sugar or eggs in baking.

Total Time: 1 hour
Serving Size: 1
Prep Time: 10 minutes
Cook Time: 50 minutes
Nutritional Facts:
per recipe
Calories: 480 kcal
Carbs: 132 g
Fat: 0 g
Protein: 0 g

Ingredients:

- 6 medium (2 lb) apples of choice, peeled and diced
- ¼ cup water, if needed
- 1 cinnamon stick (optional)

     The Science-Backed Anti-Inflammatory Diet for Beginners

Directions:

1. In a medium saucepan, add the diced apples with the optional cinnamon stick, and cook over low heat for 40–50 minutes.

2. The apples release liquid as they cook, so only add a little water if the fruit sticks to the bottom of the saucepan.

3. Remove the cinnamon stick before bottling the chunky applesauce. If you prefer a smooth applesauce, put the mixture through a blender until the preferred texture is reached.

4. Allow to fully cool before serving.

ROASTED GREEN BEANS WITH MUSHROOMS AND WALNUTS (VG, V, DF, GF, EF, NF)

This side dish brings a delicious earthy and nutty flavor to Hanukkah, and the truffle oil is known to be highly anti-inflammatory. If you don't like truffle oil, substitute it with EVOO.

Total Time: 20 minutes
Serving Size: 4
Prep Time: 5 minutes
Cook Time: 15 minutes
Nutritional Facts:
per serving
Calories: 96 kcal
Carbs: 7 g
Fat: 7 g
Protein: 4 g

Ingredients:

- ¼ cup walnuts, chopped
- 2 tsp truffle oil or EVOO
- 8 oz button mushrooms, quartered
- 8 oz green beans, trimmed and cut into 1–2 inches
- salt and pepper, to taste

Directions:

1. Preheat the oven to 400 °F.
2. To a rimmed baking sheet, add all the ingredients, except the oil, and toss lightly to cover with spices. Lightly spray with some olive oil.
3. Place in the oven and roast for 15 minutes, mixing everything halfway through.
4. Remove the mixture from the oven and add the truffle oil before serving.

EID CELEBRATION

Eid is a Muslim holiday that means the "Festival of Breaking the Fast" which occurs at the end of Ramadan.

ANJEER SHAHI TUKDA WITH ALMOND MILK (VG, V, DF, GF, EF)

Shahi tukda means the "royal piece or bite" and is a scrumptious bread pudding which is easily adaptable for all types of bread.

Total Time: 20 minutes
Serving Size: 4
Prep Time: 10 minutes
Cook Time: 10 minutes
Nutritional Facts:
per serving
Calories: 340 kcal
Carbs: 38 g
Fat: 14 g
Protein: 13 g

Ingredients:

- 1 tsp rose essence
- 1 g saffron strands
- 1 tsp manuka honey
- 1.4 oz Anjeer (dried figs)
- 1.8 oz almonds, soaked overnight

- 6.7 fl oz almond milk
- 8 slices of gluten-free bread

Directions:

1. Add the soaked almonds, dried figs, and some almond milk to a blender, and process until a smooth paste forms.
2. Pour the remaining almond milk and fig paste into a saucepan, and cook over low heat for 5 minutes until it starts thickening. Then pour in the rose water.
3. Toast the bread until lightly crisped, and then add to a plate.
4. Place the saffron strands in the warm milk mixture, and allow it to stand for a few minutes.
5. Gently spoon all the milk mixture over the bread.
6. Transfer the bread to the fridge, and let it rest until cooled before serving.

VEGETARIAN FATTEH (PITA WITH CHICKPEAS AND YOGURT) (V, GF, EF, NF)

This delicious dish is brimming with flavor thanks to the chickpeas, yogurt, and a mixture of spices. Keep it vegetarian or add meat, if you're so inclined..

Total Time: 35 minutes
Serving Size: 4
Prep Time: 15 minutes
Cook Time: 20 minutes
Nutritional Facts:
per serving
Calories: 534 kcal
Carbs: 75 g
Fat: 14 g
Protein: 32 g

Ingredients:

- ½ medium lemon, juiced
- ½ tsp nutmeg

- ½ tsp cinnamon
- ¾ bag of MorningStar Farms Veggie Grillers Crumbles
- 1 cup low-fat Greek yogurt
- 1 tbsp EVOO, more for drizzling
- 1 tbsp of pine nuts
- 1 (15 oz) can of chickpeas, rinsed
- 1 tbsp tahini
- 2 garlic cloves, minced
- 3 mini pearl onions, minced
- 4 gluten-free pitas (6 ½-inch diameter)
- kosher salt
- fresh parsley, to garnish

Directions:

1. Preheat the oven to 375 °F.
2. Cut the pita into thick strips or squares and place on a baking tray before drizzling some olive oil. Bake in the oven for about 10 minutes; they should just be crispy. Don't forget them in the oven!
3. During this time, add the yogurt, lemon juice, garlic, onions, salt, and tahini to a small bowl, and mix to an even consistency. Place in the fridge until ready to use.
4. In a frying pan, add a tablespoon of oil and bring it to a simmer. Pour in the crumbles and pine nuts, and raise the temperature to medium-high.
5. Scatter in the cinnamon and nutmeg and continue to sauté for 5 minutes.
6. On a serving plate, add the pita pieces before topping them with the yogurt mixture and scattering the chickpeas over.
7. Add the mixture from the frying pan as evenly as possible.
8. Garnish and serve.

VEGETABLE BIRYANI (V, VG, DF, GF, EF, NF)

Biryani is a must during Eid, but there is no need for meat! Enjoy this spice-filled, vegan-friendly meal that's filled with warming and anti-inflammatory spices.

Total Time: 1 hour 20 minutes

Serving Size: 8

Prep Time: 10 minutes plus 30 minutes (for soaking)

Cook Time: 40 minutes

Nutritional Facts: per serving

Calories: 310 kcal
Carbs: 57 g
Fat: 7 g
Protein: 6 g

Ingredients:

- ¼ cup cashews
- ¼ tsp black pepper
- 1 tsp salt, divided
- ½ tsp cardamom
- ½ tsp ground turmeric
- 1 (15 oz) can of chickpeas, drained and rinsed
- 1 large yellow onion, sliced thinly
- 1 small potato, cubed
- 1 tsp cinnamon
- 1 cup carrots, diced
- 1 tsp cumin
- 1 tsp chili powder
- 1 star anise
- 1 tsp ground coriander
- 1 tsp fresh ginger, grated
- 1 tsp garam masala

- 1 red bell pepper, sliced thinly
- 2 bay leaves
- 2 cups uncooked brown basmati rice
- 2 tbsp lemon juice
- 2 tbsp olive oil
- 3 tbsp coconut cream
- 4 cups veggie stock
- 5 whole cloves
- 5 garlic cloves, roughly chopped
- ½ cup raisins (optional)
- fresh cilantro or parsley (optional, for garnishing)

Directions:

1. Add the uncooked rice to a bowl and soak in water for 30 minutes before draining.

2. While the rice is soaking, add the oil and onions to a stockpot over medium heat, and cook for 5 minutes.

3. To the onions, add the cumin, star anise, pepper, bay leaves, half the salt, cardamom, cinnamon, and cloves, and cook while stirring for a minute.

4. Add the garlic and ginger, and cook for 30 seconds.

5. Place the potatoes and carrots in the mixture and cook for 2–3 minutes.

6. Add the remaining salt with the turmeric, bell pepper, coriander, cashews, chili powder, and garam masala,

and cook for 2–3 minutes while stirring.

7. Pour in the coconut cream, vegetable stock, drained rice, and chickpeas.

8. Bring the mixture to a boil while stirring, then bring to a simmer over low. Cover the stockpot, and continue to cook for 20–25 minutes, allowing the moisture to be absorbed.

9. Allow the stockpot to rest for 10 minutes covered before opening, fluffing the rice, adding the lemon juice and raisins, then stirring before serving.

TABBOULEH (VG, V, DF, EF, NF)

Tabbouleh often accompanies grilled fish or chicken but can be enjoyed by itself. While traditionally made with bulgur wheat, this can be switched out for quinoa to make it gluten-free.

Total Time: 45 minutes
Serving Size: 4
Prep Time: 45 minutes
Cook Time: no cooking required
Nutritional Facts: per serving
Calories: 259 kcal
Carbs: 14 g
Fat: 23 g
Protein: 3 g

Ingredients:

- ¼ cup fine bulgur wheat, soaked until tender, no cooking required
- ½ tsp sea salt
- 1 scallion, trimmed and sliced thinly
- 1 tbsp mint leaves, chopped finely
- 1 cup diced tomatoes
- 3 cups parsley, chopped finely
- 4 tbsp freshly squeezed lemon juice
- 6 tbsp EVOO
- freshly ground black pepper, to taste

- a pinch of cayenne, cinnamon, or seven-spice blend (optional)

Directions:

1. Once the bulgur is tender, add it to a bowl with the parsley, tomatoes, scallions, and mint.
2. Season with olive oil, pepper, lemon juice, and salt before mixing well.
3. Best served immediately or refrigerated for later in the day.

THANKSGIVING DINNER

Thanksgiving is a day of expressing gratitude and reflecting on the blessing of the year, often celebrated by Americans and Canadians.

PUMPKIN PIE BARS (DF, GF, EF, NF)

Pumpkin pie is a must-have for Thanksgiving, and these bars are just the perfect portion to prevent you from overdoing it.

Total Time: 50 minutes
Serving Size: 9
Prep Time: 10 minutes
Cook Time: 40 minutes
Nutritional Facts:
per serving
Calories: 364 kcal
Carbs: 40 g
Fat: 22 g
Protein: 4 g

Ingredients:

For the Crust

- ½ tsp baking soda
- ½ cup plus 1 tbsp coconut flour
- ½ cup coconut oil
- 1 tbsp gelatin
- 2 tbsp maple syrup
- 3 tbsp arrowroot starch

For the Filling

- ¼ cup maple syrup
- ¼ cup coconut oil, melted
- ¼ cup water
- ¼ cup coconut cream, softened
- 1 tsp cinnamon
- 1 tbsp gelatin
- 2 cups pumpkin purée

Directions:

For the Crust

1. Preheat the oven to 350 °F.
2. Prepare an 8 x 8-inch baking pan by lining it with parchment paper and greasing it with coconut oil.
3. Add all the dry ingredients into a mixing bowl and whisk together.
4. Combine the maple syrup and coconut oil until well incorporated with the dry ingredients.
5. Evenly distribute the crust in the prepared baking pan and press it down lightly.
6. Bake in the oven for 15 minutes before allowing it to cool completely.

For the Filling

1. While the crust is cooling, in a clean mixing bowl, add the cinnamon, pumpkin purée, coconut cream, coconut oil, and maple syrup, and mix until smooth.
2. Add the water to a saucepan before sprinkling the gelatin over it, and allow it to harden for 2–3 minutes.
3. Heat the gelatin mixture over low heat for 1–2 minutes, returning to a liquid state. Remove from heat and whisk vigorously until frothy.
4. Pour the froth into the pumpkin mixture and mix well.
5. Slowly pour the pumpkin mixture into the cooled crust and smooth the top.
6. Allow the pie to cool in the fridge for 3–4 hours before serving with toppings of choice.

STUFFED ACORN SQUASH (VG, V, DF, GF, EF)

For a plant-based main for Thanksgiving this year, trying stuffed acorn squash is the way to go. Not only is it a seasoned gourd, but it's stuffed to the brim with earthy, aromatic flavors, and it comes in a natural bowl.

Total Time: 1 hour
Serving Size: 4
Prep Time: 20 minutes
Cook Time: 40 minutes
Nutritional Facts:
per serving
Calories: 330 kcal
Carbs: 36 g
Fat: 16 g
Protein: 17 g

Ingredients:

- ¼ cup sage, chopped
- ⅓ cup walnuts, chopped roughly
- ⅓ cup dried cranberries
- ½ tbsp rosemary, chopped
- ½ yellow onion, chopped
- 1 tbsp apple cider vinegar
- 1 (8 oz) package of tempeh
- 1 tbsp tamari
- 1 tbsp EVOO
- 2 acorn squash, halved and deseeded
- 3 garlic cloves, minced
- 8 oz cremini mushrooms, diced
- sea salt, to taste
- freshly ground black pepper, to taste
- some parsley and a few pomegranate arils (the fleshy seeds), for garnish

Directions:

1. Preheat the oven to 425 °F.
2. Add some parchment paper to a baking tray, and place the squash cut-side up before drizzling with olive oil and seasoning with salt and pepper. Roast for 40 minutes.
3. During this time, cut the tempeh into ½-inch cubes,

and place them in a steamer basket or fine mesh strainer inside a pot with an inch of water. Allow the water to reach a simmer before covering it with a lid and allowing the tempeh to steam for 10 minutes.

4. Remove and drain excess liquid from tempeh before crumbling.

5. In a skillet, heat the olive oil over medium heat, and add the onion, some black pepper, and ½ teaspoon salt before cooking for 5 minutes.

6. Add the diced mushrooms, and cook for 8 minutes before stirring in the garlic, crumbled tempeh, sage, rosemary, walnuts, apple cider vinegar, and tamari. Allow the mixture to cook for 2–3 minutes. If the pan gets dry, add ¼ cup water.

7. Sprinkle in the cranberries before seasoning to taste.

8. Spoon the tempeh mixture equally between the acorn squashes, and garnish with pomegranates and parsley.

"CREAMED" SPINACH (VG, DF, V, GF, EF, NF)

Are you dreaming of creamed spinach, but are lactose intolerant? Try this recipe to experience the creamiest spinach without the bloat!

Total Time: 40 minutes
Serving Size: 6
Prep Time: 10 minutes
Cook Time: 30 minutes
Nutritional Facts:
per serving
Calories: 149 kcal
Carbs: 5 g
Fat: 13 g
Protein: 2 g

Ingredients:

- ¼ tsp ground nutmeg
- ½ tsp salt

- ½ tsp lemon zest
- 1 medium yellow onion,

chopped

- 1 tbsp gluten-free, all-purpose flour
- 1 ¼ cups full-fat coconut milk
- 2 tbsp avocado oil
- 4 garlic cloves, minced
- 5 oz baby spinach

Directions:

1. In a large pot over medium heat, add the oil and onions, and cook for 8–10 minutes before adding the garlic and cooking for another 2 minutes.
2. Lower the heat, and add the salt, flour, nutmeg, and zest, stirring until well combined.
3. While stirring, slowly add the coconut milk until the mixture thickens.
4. Add the spinach and continue to stir until it's well incorporated.
5. Cover the pot, and allow the spinach to cook for 3–5 minutes, allowing it to wilt. Stir again.
6. Do a taste test and spice to preference before serving.

CITRUS AND HERB-RUBBED TURKEY BREAST (GF, EF, NF)

It can take some time to prepare an entire turkey, so why do that when all you need are some turkey breasts? The combination of citrus, sage, and rosemary will help enhance the turkey taste, and you'll consume less fat by eating white meat.

Total Time:
2 hours 20 minutes

Serving Size: 6

Prep Time: 20 minutes

Cook Time: 2 hours

Nutritional Facts:
per serving

Calories: 608 kcal

Carbs: 4 g

Fat: 16 g

Protein: 110 g

- 1 tbsp fresh sage leaves, chopped finely
- 1 cup chicken stock
- 1 tbsp room temperature butter
- 1 medium orange, zested and juiced
- 1 tsp ground black pepper
- 1 small lemon, zested and juiced
- 1 tbsp fresh rosemary leaves, chopped finely
- 2 tsp salt
- 2 tbsp EVOO
- 6 lb turkey breasts

Directions:

1. Preheat the oven to 325 °F.
2. In a roasting pan, place the turkey breasts skin-side up.
3. Add the zest and juice of the lemon and orange to a small bowl with olive oil, butter, pepper, herbs, and salt, then mix until a paste forms.
4. Rub the paste over the skin of the turkey. Include some under the skin by gently lifting it; avoid tearing it.
5. Pour the stock around the turkey breasts and place the roasting pan in the oven.
6. Cook the turkey for 1 ½–2 hours until the internal temperature is 150–165 °F and the skin browns.
7. Remove the roasting pan from the oven, and cover with tinfoil, allowing the meat to rest for 15 minutes.
8. Slice the meat and serve with any accumulated juices in the pan.

Now that you're armed with many of these delicious recipes, it's time to put together an anti-inflammatory meal plan.

PART 3:

21-DAY MEAL PLAN AND HEALTH JOURNAL

It's one thing to know what you have to eat to get healthy; it's something completely different to know when to eat what. In the final section, we will look at how to create a 21-day meal plan that's unique to your needs, using the recipes in the previous section and a few other suggestions. There will even be some helpful hints on how to track your progress and keep yourself going when things start to get a little difficult.

CHAPTER 7

ACHIEVE HEALTH AND WELLNESS IN 21 DAYS

Now that you have your delicious recipes, it's time to put them to good use by designing a unique meal plan.

HOW TO USE THE MEAL PLAN

A meal plan is similar to your diet. It needs to be adaptable to your needs with various substitutions, have portion control, and be flexible enough to match the lifestyle you're living. What works for one person may not work for you. A meal plan helps you stay on track with your goals, takes the guesswork out of making daily meals, and prevents poor snacking habits.

Before considering making a meal plan, you must think about what foods you can prepare ahead of time and what can be done with minimal time needed. Go through your fridge, freezer, and pantry to see what ingredients you have, and compare them to the recipes you want to make. There is no reason to buy ingredients if they're already available.

Review a handful of recipes, and jot down any ingredients you will need to purchase to make them. Choose some of your favorite recipes and a few new ones to explore. Create a shopping list, so you know exactly what it is you need. This helps save money and keep you from wandering to other aisles in the store that could contain food you shouldn't eat. Don't discredit frozen or canned foods. They save time in preparation and come in a variety of low-salt options.

Ideally, to save time, it's a good idea to bulk buy and cook foods such as your protein, grains, and vegetables, as all can be safely frozen or stored in the fridge for three to five days. These food types can be prepared separately or as part of a meal. Regardless of how they are prepared, ensure they are all correctly portioned to go into meals or be enjoyed as part of a meal. It's far easier to defrost a portion than a whole frozen meal and then take a portion, as a meal should only be defrosted once to remain safe to eat.

Consider how you will utilize leftovers. If you're cooking a whole chicken, think of using recipes that utilize all parts of the chicken. One meal could have a thigh, while another uses shredded breast meat to top tacos, pancakes, and more. Avoid as much wastage as possible.

When building up a meal plan, start with repetitions of easy and favored meals for breakfast and lunch while allowing your snacks and dinners to bring variety. Choose what recipes best suit your taste and anti-inflammatory game plan.

IMPORTANCE OF MAINTAINING PROGRESS

Some health changes are easier to notice than others—especially when those changes are taking place inside of you. However, it helps to physically see progress being made, as that is the motivation you'll need to continue making the necessary changes.

Start with having a reasonable goal in mind. Consider weight, size (inches), decrease in inflammation symptoms, and blood pressure to name a few, as these can be self-documented. Although you could set a goal to lower inflammation markers in your blood, this will require blood tests that could be a burden on your health insurance.

Tracking and measuring these goals shows how you improve and keeps you positive about your changes over time. Don't just have an end goal, have several goals that can be achieved while reaching for that final goal. Each time a goal is achieved, celebrate. Recognize your hard work! It's gratifying to see the results in black and white. It helps prevent you from falling back on old habits.

However, to truly achieve this, you must be accountable for what you are measuring and writing down. Lying to yourself, your health journal, or your fitness or health app is only going to hurt your chances. Stay motivated to document your journey by using apps that can immediately show you how your food fuels you.

Talk to friends and family about your lifestyle changes, and show them how you are trying to improve yourself. Doing this allows your family to plan around your constraints and not peer pressure you into eating things that can damage your progress.

If weight is one of your goals, please remember that what the scale reads isn't happiness. It isn't who you are. There are many other positive steps you can take. Instead of considering the number on the scale, consider the inches lost. After all, a cubic inch of muscle weighs more than a cubic inch of fat but takes up less space. This means that you'll gain a better body condition before the scale starts dipping.

WEEKLY PLANS

Starting a meal plan can be tough—especially if you've never tried one before. To help you with creating your unique meal plan, here are three weeks' worth of meal plans with three main meals and two snack options. You can adapt it as you see fit with recipes from Chapters 3–6. Don't be afraid to play around with the ideas and switch out meals for your preferred ones.

If a 21-day meal plan seems too daunting for you, start with a single week. Bulk cook over the weekend to help prepare for the week, and see how you feel after the first week. Don't assume you'll be magically cured after a single week; this is to only mentally prepare you for the changes that will occur after a few weeks. However, by completing the first week, you'll know what foods you prefer over others or may be open to trying new recipes. Whatever the reason, start slow and build yourself up to completing a full 21-day anti-inflammatory meal plan.

Week 1	Meal 1	Meal 2	Meal 3	Snack 1	Snack 2
Day 1	Lemon–berry ricotta toast	Turmeric chicken with some green beans and a baked potato	Ginger salmon with roasted green beans	A cup of blueberries	Peanut butter energy balls
Day 2	Almond flour pancakes topped with berries of choice	Chickpea and quinoa bowl	Turkey balls on a bed of preferred greens	Cheesy green frittata	Medium carrot with ¼ cup hummus
Day 3	Spinach and mushroom egg bites with smoothie of choice	Ginger beef stir-fry	Brisket and roots	A cup of cucumber with some guacamole	Baked oatmeal
Day 4	Gourmet avocado toast	Chickpea pasta with mushrooms and kale	Chickpea and quinoa bowl	Carrot–apple smoothie	A cup of different colored bell peppers
Day 5	Lemon–berry yogurt toast	Turmeric chicken with crispy potatoes	Brisket with sweet potato latkes	An ounce of dark chocolate	Gourmet avocado toast
Day 6	Strawberry and yogurt parfait	Ginger–tahini salmon bake	Vegetable biryani	Mixed berry breakfast smoothie	Half a cup of Greek yogurt and raspberries
Day 7	Banana muffins with fruit of choice	Pea soup with a slice of gluten-free bread	Chickpea pasta with mushrooms and kale	15 unsalted almonds	Almond flour pancakes with berries of choice

Now that the first week is over, reevaluate your meals as needed or continue onto the second week.

Week 2	Meal 1	Meal 2	Meal 3	Snack 1	Snack 2
Day 1	Baked oatmeal	Beet and shrimp salad	Brisket and roots	Almond flour pancakes topped with berries of choice	Whole wheat English muffin with a tablespoon of peanut butter
Day 2	Chickpea omelet	Turmeric chicken with Tunisian salad	Gourmet avocado toast	A cup of edamame (as is or tossed with half a teaspoon of EVOO)	Cinnamon baked apples
Day 3	Breakfast salad	Lamb and beef balti with a side of kale, spinach, or collard greens	Chickpea and quinoa bowl	Banana muffin	An ounce of cheese and a medium pear
Day 4	Spinach and feta scrambled egg pitas	Chickpea pasta with mushrooms and kale	Vegetable biryani with roasted green beans, mushrooms, and walnuts	A cup of cherries and some pumpkin hummus	Berry–kefir smoothie
Day 5	Honey-roasted cherry and ricotta tartine	Baked branzino with Tunisian salad	Pea soup with a slice of gluten-free bread	Peanut butter energy balls	8 whole wheat crackers and a quarter cup hummus
Day 6	Cheesy green frittata	Stuffed acorn squash with creamed spinach	Turkey balls with crispy oven-roasted potatoes	A cup of preferred raw veggies with guacamole	Blackberry smoothie
Day 7	Quinoa and chia oatmeal mix served with nuts of choice	Heart chili	Citrus and herb-rubbed turkey breast with a side salad	A portion of lemon–blueberry poke cake	Pumpkin pie bar with coconut cream

The Science-Backed Anti-Inflammatory Diet for Beginners

If you feel more comfortable, create your own third-week meal plan, or make use of the last meal plan.

Week 3	Meal 1	Meal 2	Meal 3	Snack 1	Snack 2
Day 1	Avocado and smoked salmon omelet	Goat cheese sandwich with arugula and pickled beets	Stuffed acorn squash and tabbouleh	A piece of yogurt bark with half a cup of berries	Cheesy green frittata
Day 2	Spinach and feta scrambled egg pitas	Hearty chili	Grilled chicken breast with green beans almondine	Spinach–avocado smoothie	A portion of lemon–blueberry poke cake
Day 3	Avocado and smoked trout breakfast salad	Chickpea and quinoa bowl	Ratatouille with an egg	A portion of apple crisp with cranberries	Date and pine nut overnight oats
Day 4	Baked oatmeal	Pea soup with a slice of gluten-free bread	Quinoa Mediterranean salad	Whole wheat English muffin with a tablespoon of peanut butter	A portion of lemon–blueberry nice cream topped with a handful of almonds
Day 5	Fancy egg sandwiches	Baked branzino with tabbouleh	Ratatouille with an egg	Peanut butter and jelly smoothie	An ounce of dark chocolate
Day 6	Raspberry–peach–mango smoothie bowl	Gourmet avocado toast	Ginger–tahini salmon bake	Peanut butter energy balls	Mango–almond smoothie bowl
Day 7	Breakfast burrito	Greek salad with edamame and fatty fish of choice	Chickpea and quinoa bowl	Spinach and mushroom egg bites	A portion of lemon–blueberry nice cream topped with preferred berries.

If you feel more comfortable, create your own third-week meal plan, or make use of the last meal plan.

PREPARATION TIPS

The key to a successful meal plan is the preparation. Being prepared ahead of a meal makes it easier to have more time to do what you want to do in the evening instead of sitting and contemplating dinner and then opting to get a pizza.

The first plan of action is to gather the recipes you want to try for the week or the duration of the meal plan and craft a shopping list. Inspect your pantry to ensure you're only purchasing what's needed. Next, ensure that you have enough containers that are microwavable or freezer-safe to store any meals you want for the week. Ideally, these containers should be large enough to hold a single portion. Alternatively, food can be portioned into individual plastic bags and then frozen or stored in a container.

Bulk cook meals or portions of meals on days when you have time to spare. Cook three to five full meals, while planning to have ingredients for quick meals in the fridge. Ready-to-use ingredients, such as cut and prepared vegetables, can be stored in the fridge until required and save a lot of time when you're in the middle of a recipe. In addition, ready-cut fruits and vegetables can be portioned and used as snacks.

Consider having a few easy recipes scattered throughout the meal plan for nights when you know you're going to be busy. Nothing says you have to have a cooked meal at dinnertime. Some overnight oats can be just as filling at night as it is in the morning, and it takes minutes to put together.

Repurpose leftovers. Learn to never throw food out, as there are a variety of ways to repurpose anything left over from a meal. Some leftover meat or vegetables go well as a filling inside an omelet, or you could consider making a charcuterie board to avoid cooking. Remember, your meal plan is adaptable. If you want to cook one night, then cook. However, if you are exhausted and your fridge is already stocked with leftovers, then make use of them!

Get the whole family involved. If you're a parent, or a young adult who has dependents in the house, get them involved in meal preparation. A family that cooks together stays healthy together and may even surprise you with a prepared dinner on nights you're too exhausted to think. Work together on weekends to prepare various recipes and ingredients, treating all the helpers to a delicious meal with a tasty treat at the end.

At the end of the day, a change in diet and lifestyle is more than just planning, having a meal plan in place, and tracking your daily habits. You also need to consider your feelings associated with the journey you're taking. In the next chapter, we'll discuss the benefits of keeping a health journal and how it will benefit your well-being.

CHAPTER 8

THE HEALTH JOURNAL

There are many reasons journaling can help you on your quest to get healthier. Journaling helps people find inspiration, lowers stress and anxiety, and even bolsters self-confidence. It's truly one of the best ways to reflect on yourself and be the mirror of your health's soul.

DAILY LOG FOR DIET AND WATER INTAKE

It doesn't matter if you're a paper-and-pen kind of person or someone more in tune with technology; logging what you eat and drink is the best way to monitor what is going into your body.

By keeping a log, you're holding yourself accountable, which in turn will increase your success rate, but only if you're honest with yourself. How you record your intake is completely up to you. Many apps, such as MyFitnessPal, Noom, PlateJoy, and even MyPlate Calorie Counter, can all record what you're consuming to various degrees. Some features may require you to pay a monthly or yearly subscription, while other apps can be used without the unnecessary features. You will need to weigh the pros and cons of each to determine what is best for you. The advantage of the apps over pen and paper is that you can generally see the nutritional information as soon as the food or drink is added. However, that isn't to say you have to use them.

If you have a good idea of the nutrients in your food and you're happy to journal, then consider a table, like the one below, to add when you eat and drink various foods. You can even break down the timeline into individual hours. This will be better if you're trying to drink more water daily. Dehydration is one of the causes of constipation, which can affect your gut health.

Getting enough water into your body can be tricky, especially when active or living in an area with high temperatures.

Many apps that monitor food consumption could also be used for tracking how much water you drink. There are even some fitness watches that do this! On average, men need 127 ounces of liquid a day, and women roughly 91 ounces (Jewell, 2023). However, many foods also contribute to this fluid intake. Taking this into account, men will need to drink roughly 101 ounces (12 and a half cups) of water, and women will need 74 ounces (just over 9 cups).

The best way to get enough to drink is to consume a cup or two of water before starting your day, as well as drink a cup of water before and after each meal. Some people like to have a timer set for when they must drink, while others have a reusable bottle of water that has markings on it to remind the person when they need to drink.

Whatever method you use, be sure to make your drinking experience fun! You don't have to stick to plain water. Herb, spice, and fruit-infused water is not only tasty but also has bonuses from what you put in it. Too cold to drink water? Heat the water and sip away at it throughout the day.

PAIN SCALE

With inflammation comes pain, whether that's from arthritis (joint inflammation) or digestive issues (gut inflammation). Tracking pain levels from inflammatory conditions can help indicate whether the anti-inflammatory diet is working for you. However, as with diets, everyone's pain scale is different. What could be minor to you could be significantly more painful to someone else.

This is why you should develop a pain scale that is unique to you. You can do this by creating a scale from 0–10, with 0 being no pain and 10 being the most excruciating pain you can imagine. You can then compare any painful feelings to what you view as the most excruciating and determine a scale that works for you.

It can be as simple as:

- 0: No pain

- 1–3: Mild pain (annoying but you can still function)

- 4–6: Moderate pain (more noticeable and it's starting to affect the way you function)

- 7–10: Severe pain (progressive pain, unable to function, and the pain is all-consuming)

You can even go into more detail, such as:

- 1: Mild (barely noticeable, and you barely think about it)

- 2: Minor (occasional and annoying sharp pain that disappears quickly)

- 3: Moderate (more noticeable and could be distracting, but you get used to it)

Use unique wording to describe your pain. It'll make it easier to describe to a physician if required.

GUT MONITORING

Pain isn't the only factor you can monitor. How you digest your food can also be a good indicator of the diet working. A healthy gut means you shouldn't be suffering from bloating, gas, or other disruptive digestion issues.

A few great ways you can check your gut health include monitoring the regularity of bowel movements (compared to what is the norm for you), observing the color of the bowel movements, noting whether there is gas present, identifying if there is pain or straining, and tracking the transition time.

Ideally, a bowel movement should be soft-firm, medium to dark brown, and smooth and should sink once it hits the water. The food eaten should take 24–48 hours to travel through the digestive tract. Anything deviating from this can be an indication of a digestive problem.

In most cases, a little gas now and again isn't bad, but when trapped, it can cause discomfort, pain, and bloating. To avoid this, consider eating fewer foods that produce gas, such as cruciferous vegetables.

Color is also a good indication that something may be wrong.

- Pale greenish-yellow: Poor absorption or bile duct issues

- Black or red: Internal bleeding or beet-rich diet

- Green: A diet high in vegetables that aren't digesting well (note: cook vegetables thoroughly)

- • Yellow: A possible sign of infection

Stools that float tend to have a higher fat content. Lower your fat intake and see if there is an improvement. If there isn't, you may need a doctor to inspect your bile ducts and liver.

If you are unsure how long it takes for food to go through your digestive tract, eat a large meal of beets. A red bowel movement will let you know that the beets have completed their journey. Take note of this.

Bloating can be caused by a variety of factors, some of them include sensitivities, intolerances, gastroparesis (causes food movement to slow down), and even small intestinal bacterial overgrowth (SIBO) which will need to be identified by a doctor.

Thankfully, there are many ways to help get rid of bloating. The first is to keep an accurate food diary, so you can determine what food may be causing the problem. Learn to eat mindfully. Eat slower, taking smaller bites and chewing thoroughly to avoid swallowing air. Taking probiotic supplements can alleviate many gut discomforts, including bloating. You can even try to eat smaller meals and get more active to help the digestive process. Whatever you try, be sure to add it to your journal so you can see what works best for you.

HUNGER SCALE

Many of us have forgotten that our body tells us that we are full. Some people are indoctrinated to clean their plates, while others binge because they tend to skip meals. Due to this, they have forgotten that the body has cues—thanks to the hypothalamus—to let you know when you're hungry or full.

To help you learn about your body cues, create a hunger scale with a range of 1–10 or what you're comfortable with. A rating of 1 means that you are starving and physically feel ill from not eating. Meanwhile, a rating of 10 means you are physically ill as you have overeaten.

- • A rating of 1–3 means you are too hungry.

- • A rating of 4 means you are hungry and should have a meal.

- • A rating of 5 is neutral; you could still feel hungry but don't need an immediate meal.

- A rating of 6–7 means you're starting to feel satisfied and should stop eating.

- A rating of 8 means you're starting to get uncomfortably full.

- A rating of 9 and higher means you feel bloated and have eaten too much.

To prevent you from reaching a rating of 8 or higher, practice mindful eating. Chew slowly and concentrate on your meal. Once you think your hunger scale is reaching a 6, take 15 minutes of not eating anymore to see if you're still hungry or not. Continue if you are, or stop if you're not.

This rating system is not a hard and fast rule, each person is different, and you should determine your own scale for what works best for you. The important thing is that you listen to your body to establish a healthy relationship with it.

Here is an example of what your journal page should look like.

Meal 1	Water intake
Meal 2	Exercise
Meal 3	Pain scale
Snack 1	Gut Color: Consistency: Regularity: Other symptoms:
Snack 2	

If there are other aspects of your life that you want to monitor, tweak the example to best suit your needs.

REFLECTION AND FUTURE PLANNING

A diet is only good if it is something that can be done long enough to be a lifestyle change for the better. Any slip from the diet and reintroducing of inflammatory foods will result in inflammation occurring once again. To prevent this from occurring, take the time to reflect on how far you have come in your progress. Think about all the changes you have made to reach this point and how you have improved your health.

Recognize the work you put in and the progress you have made. Learn from any mistake you have made and milestones you have reached. This isn't about mistakes you have made but improvements you can make and identifying areas that still need improvements, allowing you to become self-aware of the journey you have undertaken. Concentrate on the positives, and update your journal with your triumphs, dips, and feelings you have experienced along the way.

How to Maintain an Anti-Inflammatory Lifestyle

Sticking with something new can be tough, but with positive reinforcement over time, something new will become a habit. The longer you work at something, the better and easier it becomes over time. Here are a few handy tips to get you to stay the course:

- Ease into it.
- Try new whole foods, especially vegetables and grains. Sneak vegetables into your food where you can (snacks, smoothies, and so on).
- Explore different lean meat options and increase your seafood intake.
- Try a few plant-based meals to replace meat-heavy meals.
- Learn how to control portion size.
- Learn to read ingredient lists and know your sensitivities.
- Adapt the diet to suit your needs, eating foods you enjoy.

- Have snacks ready.

- If eating out, plan and review the menu. Don't be afraid to ask for sauces on the side.

- Limit or remove poor foods from your vicinity.

- Don't skip meals.

- Have snacks ready.

- Keep journaling.

- Patience!

- A slipup isn't a failure; it's an opportunity to reevaluate yourself and improve.

With that, you have learned everything you need to know about how to carefully construct an anti-inflammatory diet that suits your every need. While each chapter has vital information, it is by no means an outline that will suit all your needs. Take what you have learned and take back your life from painful inflammation.

CONCLUSION

Chronic inflammation is the leading cause of death in modern humans. Diseases such as stroke, heart disease, diabetes, arthritis, and more all start because of inflammation. While inflammation is needed by the body, as it's a response to potentially harmful infections and invasions of bacteria and viruses, if the inflammation continues for too long, it can cause a cascade of problems.

One of the best ways to combat inflammation is by looking at what you consume. After all, food is what fuels your body, but it first needs to be digested before this can occur. When continually eating foods that are pro-inflammatory, such as foods high in red or processed meat, salt, and saturated fats, the body responds to it the same way it would an invader. Over time, the body will start attacking itself, leading to digestive issues, lower diversity in the gut microbiome, and the possibility of developing a leaky gut, which causes a wider range of problems when undigested food and intestinal contents leak out.

However, changing a lifetime of poor eating can be difficult—especially when you don't have any guidance. Not everyone has the medical or dietary know-how to understand what is online or whether it's fact or false. The best thing you can do for your health is to take the time to educate yourself about the foods that can cause inflammatory responses and cut them from your life. However, it's not that easy.

While allergies are easily identified, usually during childhood, sensitivities and intolerances can develop over time, and they can be difficult to figure out. Thankfully, with all the knowledge accumulated from this book, you're now able to identify sensitivities that are unique to you, allowing you to cut these foods from your diet without having to compromise on the goodness of an anti-inflammatory diet. Not only that, but the lessons learned will help you create a unique diet that benefits you.

The internet and various books are full of diet plans that will help lower inflammation, but these are general guidelines and can't always be specific for what you need. Being able to identify sensitivities, find alternatives for ingredients from recipes, and cook what makes you feel better each time you eat is the goal of this book.

While doctors can guide you in making decisions about improving your health, they cannot force you to take their advice. Learning to take care of yourself by improving what you eat is the first step needed to fight back against inflammation. Everything taught throughout this book aims to get you to choose what you put on your plate to help lower inflammation. Whether you're trying to eat more fish and vegetables or you're aiming to lose a few inches, an anti-inflammatory diet designed by you and for you is the best route to take. After all, you're more likely to listen to yourself than you are to anyone else.

The key to your health is in your hands, but it is only the start. There are countless delicious recipes and alternative ingredients you can explore and use as you take your anti-inflammatory journey. This is but a guide to help you on your way. Take the lessons each chapter teaches and create a new lifestyle free from pain and digestive concerns. An anti-inflammatory lifestyle is more than just a diet change, it's a revamp to your life, one where you are being healed by what is put on your plate.

So go out and get a journal to start your journey. Choose some of your favorite recipes and use the 21-day meal plan to help guide your body back from the edge of chronic inflammation. Explore different foods to find those that best suit your new anti-inflammatory lifestyle. You have nothing to lose except for the pain and the increased risk of a chronic disease that has a high chance of making your life miserable.

You aren't alone in this journey. Right now, there are thousands, if not more, of people who are struggling to decide if an anti-inflammatory diet is for them. To help them take control of their future health, please take the time to leave a review of this book to help guide them in choosing to create a unique anti-inflammatory diet that will brighten their day and improve their health.

DEDICATION

Dear Liam and Olivia,

We draw immense inspiration from both of you in our journey towards a healthier life. Our commitment to this path is not only for our own well-being but also to be present for every moment you grow, flourish, and chase your dreams. We love you like all little children love pennies. You are at the center of our world.

Love Always,
Mommy and Daddy

The Recipe for Resilience

Dear Reader,

As you turn the pages of "The Science Backed Anti-Inflammatory Diet for Beginners," you're doing more than just reading—you're equipping yourself with the knowledge to make transformative choices for your health.

Remember the ancient wisdom of Hippocrates: "Let food be thy medicine and medicine be thy food." This guide is a testament to that philosophy, aiming to give you both the culinary tools and the scientific insights necessary to quell the fires of inflammation that simmer beneath many health issues.

We've carefully blended complex nutritional science with practical, actionable steps, much like a cherished recipe handed down and perfected over time. The principles within these pages are meant to be shared, to extend the health benefits you experience to others.

In your hands lies not just a book but a blueprint for resilience. And as you have been a student of this science, you can now become a teacher of it. By sharing your experience, your struggles, and triumphs, you join a community dedicated to improving health one meal at a time.

By leaving a review on platforms like Amazon you provide a beacon for fellow seekers on this path of wellness. Each review, each story, adds to the collective wisdom that informs and inspires those just beginning their journey.

Here's how you can continue to be an advocate for health:

If you are on audible-hit the three dots in the top right of your device and click rate and review, then leave a few sentences about the book with a star rating

If you are reading on kindle or an e-reader-scroll to the bottom of the book then swipe up and it will prompt a review for you.

If for some reason these changed- you can go to Amazon (or wherever you purchased this) and leave a review right on the book's page

For paperback readers- Scan the QR code below to share your review.

If all else fails scan this QR code

Your voice is powerful. Your story, a guidepost. And your insights, invaluable. Together, we create a tapestry of well-being, each review another thread that strengthens the whole.

Thank you for your invaluable support and for being a pivotal part of this movement towards collective health and resilience.

With gratitude,
Dr. Yasmine Elamir MD and Dr. William Grist MD

Congratulations on completing your journey through "The Science Backed Anti-Inflammatory Diet for Beginners." Now, you're equipped not just with recipes but with a blueprint for health that extends far beyond the dinner table.

It's incredible, isn't it? How each choice at the grocery store, each meal you prepare, can be a step toward healing. But the journey doesn't end with the last page—because now, you have a chance to be a beacon for others.

Think of your review on Amazon as a seed you plant, one that can grow into knowledge and health for others. Your honest words can shine a light for those still navigating the shadowy paths of inflammation and discomfort, showing them a way towards comfort and wellness.

By sharing your thoughts, you water the seeds of understanding, allowing the tree of collective health to grow and flourish. Each review, each story, each piece of advice adds to the canopy that shelters others on their health journey.

So please, take a moment to reflect and then share. Your experiences are the soil from which others can draw strength and sustenance.

Thank you, from the roots to the highest leaf, for not only embracing the anti-inflammatory lifestyle but for helping spread its profound benefits. Together, we're not just sowing seeds—we're cultivating a forest of wellbeing that will provide nourishment and shelter for generations to come.

With gratitude and hope for the future of our health,
Dr. Yasmine Elamir, MD and Dr. William Grist MD

REFERENCES

Ajmera, R. (2022, October 14). *A dietitian's picks of the 10 best nutrition apps to download.* Healthline. https://www.healthline.com/nutrition/top-iphone-android-apps

Ajmera, R. (2023, August 15). *Do food sensitivity tests work? What you need to know.* Healthline. https://www.healthline.com/health/food-sensitivity-test

Akers, R. (2023, January 3). *What causes abdominal bloating?* Medical News Today. https://www.medicalnewstoday.com/articles/321869

Al Bander, Z., Nitert, M. D., Mousa, A., & Naderpoor, N. (2020). The gut microbiota and inflammation: An overview. *International Journal of Environmental Research and Public Health*, 17(20). https://doi.org/10.3390/ijerph17207618

Allurion. (n.d.). *The importance of tracking your weight loss progress.* https://www.allurion.com/en/blog/importance-tracking-your-weight-loss-progress

American College of Allergy, Asthma, & Immunology. (2020, October 30). *Food allergy testing and diagnosis.* https://acaai.org/allergies/testing-diagnosis/food-allergy-testing-and-diagnosis/

annbrown. (2022a, April 5). *National taco day | Anti-inflammatory Mexican.* Vitality Consultants. https://vitalityconsultantsllc.com/national-taco-day/

annbrown. (2022b, April 21). *Paleo stuffed burger with sweet potato fries.* Vitality Consultants. https://vitalityconsultantsllc.com/stuffed-burger-with-sweet-potato-fries/

annbrown. (2022c, April 21). *Simple and healthy ways to liven up your kitchen.* Vitality Consultants. https://vitalityconsultantsllc.com/simple-and-healthy-ways-to-liven-up-your-kitchen/

Australian Eggs. (n.d.). *The health benefits of eggs.* https://www.australianeggs.org.au/nutrition/health-benefits

Axe, J. (2020, November 10). *Almond flour pancakes recipe.* Dr. Axe. https://draxe.com/recipes/almond-flour-pancakes/

Backes, M. (2022, June 2). *From the heart to the table, the benefits of homemade sauces*. Circle B Ranch and Marina. https://circlebranchpork.com/blogs/marinas-kitchen-blogs/from-the-heart-to-the-table-the-benefits-of-homemade-sauces

Balance. (2023, March 13). *7 foods to eat more of during the menopause*. https://www.balance-menopause.com/menopause-library/7-foods-to-eat-more-of-during-the-menopause/

Bashinsky, R. (2023a, September 19). *Lamb & beef balti*. EatingWell. https://www.eatingwell.com/recipe/281442/lamb-beef-balti/

Bashinsky, R. (2023b, September 19). *Mediterranean quinoa salad*. EatingWell. https://www.eatingwell.com/recipe/278401/mediterranean-quinoa-salad/

Bedosky, L. (2023, October 2). *Meal planning 101: A complete beginner's guide to meal prep*. Everyday Health. https://www.everydayhealth.com/diet-nutrition/meal-planning/

Bemis, A. (2023, September 19). *Honey-roasted cherry & ricotta tartine*. EatingWell. https://www.eatingwell.com/recipe/254592/honey-roasted-cherry-ricotta-tartine/

Bernard, L. (2023, September 24). *One pot vegetable biryani*. Make It Dairy Free. https://makeitdairyfree.com/one-pot-vegetable-biryani/

Boyers, L. (2022, December 6). *Anti-inflammatory diet: Foods to eat, avoid & A sample meal plan*. Mindbodygreen. https://www.mindbodygreen.com/articles/anti-inflammatory-diet-meal-plan

Brantley, A. (2019, April 5). *Candied sweet potato latkes*. Everyday Maven. https://www.everydaymaven.com/candied-sweet-potato-latkes

Brunt, D. (2023, March 31). *The best anti-inflammatory diet for menopause*. Otepoti. https://www.otepotiintegrativehealth.co.nz/post/the-best-anti-inflammatory-diet-for-menopause

Carver-Carter, R. (2022, July 28). *The microbiota-immune axis: How do gut bacteria influence immune health?* Atlas Blog. https://atlasbiomed.com/blog/the-microbiota-immune-axis/

Casner, C. (2018, June 8). *Quinoa & chia oatmeal mix.* EatingWell. https://www.eatingwell.com/recipe/255762/quinoa-chia-oatmeal-mix/

Casner, C. (2023a, September 9). *Baked oatmeal with banana, raisins & walnuts.* EatingWell. https://www.eatingwell.com/recipe/278299/baked-oatmeal-banana-raisins-walnuts/

Casner, C. (2023b, September 19). *Chickpea & quinoa bowl with roasted red pepper sauce.* EatingWell. https://www.eatingwell.com/recipe/258195/chickpea-quinoa-bowl-with-roasted-red-pepper-sauce/

Casner, C. (2023c, September 19). *Strawberry-chocolate Greek yogurt bark.* EatingWell. https://www.eatingwell.com/recipe/259080/strawberry-chocolate-greek-yogurt-bark/

Casner, C. (2023d, September 20). *Lemon-blueberry nice cream.* EatingWell. https://www.eatingwell.com/recipe/7981785/lemon-blueberry-nice-cream/

Casner, C. (2023e, September 20). *Lemon-Blueberry poke cake.* EatingWell. https://www.eatingwell.com/recipe/7994194/lemon-blueberry-poke-cake/

Casner, C. (2023f, September 20). *Pickled beet, arugula & herbed goat cheese sandwich.* EatingWell. https://www.eatingwell.com/recipe/7994089/pickled-beet-arugula-herbed-goat-cheese-sandwich/

Christala. (2023, February 20). *Branzino Mediterranean.* Allrecipes. https://www.allrecipes.com/recipe/236932/branzino-mediterranean/

Cirino, E. (2018, September 18). *Pain scale.* Healthline. https://www.healthline.com/health/pain-scale

Clancy, J. (2023a, September 19). *Avocado & smoked salmon omelet.* EatingWell. https://www.eatingwell.com/recipe/259657/avocado-smoked-salmon-omelet/

Clancy, J. (2023b, September 19). *Mango-almond smoothie bowl.* EatingWell. https://www.eatingwell.com/recipe/259663/mango-almond-smoothie-bowl/

Clem, J., & Barthel, B. (2021). A look at plant-based diets. *Missouri Medicine, 118*(3), 233–238. https://www.ncbi.nlm.nih.gov/pmc/articles/PMC8210981/

Cleveland Clinic. (2021, July 28). *Inflammation: What is it, causes, symptoms & treatment.* https://my.clevelandclinic.org/health/symptoms/21660-inflammation

Corleone, J. (2022, September 28). *7-Day anti-inflammatory meal plan: Recipes & prep.* Verywell Fit. https://www.verywellfit.com/7-day-anti-inflammatory-meal-plan-and-recipe-prep-6740018

Dalkin, G. (2023, September 19). *Really green smoothie.* EatingWell. https://www.eatingwell.com/recipe/270514/really-green-smoothie/

Dansky, L. (2023a, September 18). *Kale & shaved Brussels sprouts salad with avocado Caesar dressing.* EatingWell. https://www.eatingwell.com/recipe/8037997/kale-shaved-brussels-sprouts-salad-with-avocado-caesar-dressing/

Dansky, L. (2023b, September 19). *Carrot-apple smoothie.* EatingWell. https://www.eatingwell.com/recipe/7879814/carrot-apple-smoothie/

Donofrio, J. (2020, November 15). *Stuffed acorn squash.* Love and Lemons. https://www.loveandlemons.com/stuffed-acorn-squash

Dr. Myers Staff. (2023, May 16). *The best natural sweeteners for an autoimmune diet.* Amy Myers MD. https://www.amymyersmd.com/article/natural-sweeteners-aip-diet

Eagle, R. (2023, September 18). *At-home food sensitivity tests 2023: Are they reliable?* Medical News Today. https://www.medicalnewstoday.com/articles/food-sensitivity-test

EatingWell Test Kitchen. (2019, August 16). *Almond butter & banana protein smoothie.* EatingWell. https://www.eatingwell.com/recipe/251254/almond-butter-banana-protein-smoothie/

EatingWell Test Kitchen. (2022, September 15). *Pea soup.* EatingWell. https://www.eatingwell.com/recipe/249993/pea-soup/

EatingWell Test Kitchen. (2023a, September 19). *Braised brisket & roots.* EatingWell. https://www.eatingwell.com/recipe/248735/braised-brisket-roots/

EatingWell Test Kitchen. (2023b, September 19). *Date & pine nut overnight oatmeal.* EatingWell. https://www.eatingwell.com/recipe/269833/date-pine-nut-overnight-oatmeal/

EatingWell Test Kitchen. (2023c, September 19). *Egg sandwiches with rosemary, tomato & feta.* EatingWell. https://www.eatingwell.com/recipe/262836/egg-sandwiches-with-rosemary-tomato-feta/

EatingWell Test Kitchen. (2023d, September 19). *Strawberry & yogurt parfait.* EatingWell. https://www.eatingwell.com/recipe/250955/strawberry-yogurt-parfait/

EatingWell Test Kitchen. (2023e, September 20). *Avocado toast with egg, spinach & salsa.* EatingWell. https://www.eatingwell.com/recipe/251334/avocado-toast-with-egg-spinach-salsa/

EatingWell Test Kitchen. (2023f, September 20). *Baby kale breakfast salad with smoked trout & avocado.* EatingWell. https://www.eatingwell.com/recipe/251411/baby-kale-breakfast-salad-with-smoked-trout-avocado/

EatingWell Test Kitchen. (2023g, September 20). *Beet & shrimp winter salad.* EatingWell. https://www.eatingwell.com/recipe/251312/beet-shrimp-winter-salad/

Edjoukou, Y. (2023, February 27). *The benefits of tracking progress and measuring success in weight loss.* LinkedIn. https://www.linkedin.com/pulse/benefits-tracking-progress-measuring-success-weight-edjoukou-phd/

Environmental Health and Safety. (n.d.). *Health benefits of fish.* Washington State Department of Health. https://doh.wa.gov/community-and-environment/food/fish/health-benefits

Familydoctor.org Editorial Staff. (2023, May 9). *Nutrition: Keeping a food diary.* Familydoctor.org. https://familydoctor.org/nutrition-keeping-a-food-diary/

Farthing, T. (2023, September 19). *Apple crisp with cranberries.* EatingWell. https://www.eatingwell.com/recipe/268744/apple-crisp-with-cranberries/

Felman, A. (2023, April 14). *Everything you need to know about inflammation.* Medical News Today. https://www.medicalnewstoday.com/articles/248423

Fida. (2023, September 2). *Lebanese tabbouleh*. Sweet and SavouryPursuits.https://www.sweetandsavourypursuits. com/tabbouleh/

Fletcher, J. (2023, September 6). *Anti-inflammatory diet: What to know*. Medical News Today. https://www. medicalnewstoday.com/articles/320233

Frostick, J. (2023, May 11). *Tailoring meal plans to individual needs: How to create a customized diet for your unique lifestyle*. LinkedIn. https://www.linkedin.com/pulse/ tailoring-meal-plans-individual-needs-how-create- diet-frostick/

Furman, D., Campisi, J., Verdin, E., Carrera-Bastos, P., Targ, S., Franceschi, C., Ferrucci, L., Gilroy, D. W., Fasano, A., Miller, G. W., Miller, A. H., Mantovani, A., Weyand, C. M., Barzilai, N., Goronzy, J. J., Rando, T. A., Effros, R. B., Lucia, A., Kleinstreuer, N., & Slavich, G. M. (2019). Chronic inflammation in the etiology of disease across the life span. *Nature Medicine*, 25(12), 1822–1832. https://doi. org/10.1038/s41591-019-0675-0

FutureLearn. (2022, October 25). *Tailoring nutritional guidelines to suit individuals*. https://www.futurelearn. com/info/courses/food-as-medicine/0/steps/15156

Genova Diagnostics. (n.d.). *Elimination diet guide [fact sheet]*. https://www.gdx.net/core/supplemental-education- materials/Elimination-Diet-Handout.pdf

Gralow, A. (2023, August 28). *Slata tounsiya (Tunisian salad)*. The Mediterranean Dish. https://www. themediterraneandish.com/tunisian-salad-slata- tounsiya/

Grimes, L. (2022, November 10). *Pumpkin hummus*. BBC Good Food. https://www.bbcgoodfood.com/recipes/ pumpkin-houmous

Haas, S. (2023, September 19). *Ginger-tahini oven-baked salmon & vegetables*. EatingWell. https://www. eatingwell.com/recipe/274850/ginger-tahini-oven- baked-salmon-vegetables/

Hanley, R. (2018, December 12). *The exact anti-inflammatory diet meal plan that changed my life*. Ryan Hanley. https://ryanhanley.com/anti-inflammatory-diet-meal- plan/

Hartley, R. (2023, January 2). *How to use the hunger fullness scale in intuitive eating*. Rachael Hartley Nutrition. https://www.rachaelhartleynutrition.com/blog/2015/02/hunger-and-fullness-cues

Harvard Health Publishing. (2021, November 16). *Foods that fight inflammation*. https://www.health.harvard.edu/staying-healthy/foods-that-fight-inflammation

Harvard Health Publishing. (2023, April 15). *Quick-start guide to an anti-inflammation diet*. https://www.health.harvard.edu/staying-healthy/quick-start-guide-to-an-antiinflammation-diet

Harvard School of Public Health. (2019, November 4). *Whole grains*. https://www.hsph.harvard.edu/nutritionsource/what-should-you-eat/whole-grains/

Harvard School of Public Health. (2023, February 2). Diet review: *Anti-Inflammatory diet*. https://www.hsph.harvard.edu/nutritionsource/healthy-weight/diet-reviews/anti-inflammatory-diet/

Health & Wellbeing North Ward. (2018, October 24). *Why is nutrition important*. https://www.hwb.com.au/why-is-nutrition-important/

Healthwise Staff. (2022, February 23). *Pain rating scale*. Government of Alberta. https://myhealth.alberta.ca/Health/Pages/conditions.aspx?hwid=stp1310&

Hendley, J. (2023, September 19). *Fruit energy balls*. EatingWell. https://www.eatingwell.com/recipe/270496/fruit-energy-balls/

Herbert-Smith, K. (2023, March 27). *The importance of self-reflection*. IRIS Connect. https://blog.irisconnect.com/uk/community/blog/importance-of-self-reflection/

Hill, A. (2020, August 20). *How to meal plan: 23 helpful tips*. Healthline. https://www.healthline.com/nutrition/meal-prep-tips

Hoover, M. (2019a, May 30). *4 ways to test your gut health*. Unbound Wellness. https://unboundwellness.com/4-ways-test-gut-health/

Hoover, M. (2019b, September 4). *Paleo pumpkin pie bars (AIP)*. Unbound Wellness. https://unboundwellness.com/paleo-pumpkin-pie-bars-aip

INTEGRIS Health. (2017, December 14). *Anti-Inflammatory recipes for the holidays.* https://integrisok.com/resources/on-your-health/2017/december/anti-inflammatory-recipes-for-the-holidays

itsjdieb. (2021, December 19). *Vegetarian fatteh (pita with chickpeas & yogurt).* Average Arab Girl. https://www.averagearabgirl.com/post/vegetarian-fatteh-pita-with-chickpeas-yogurt

Jessica. (2020, September 21). The importance of quality meat. *The Healthy Hippie.* http://thehealthyhippieblog.com/2019/12/17/the-importance-of-quality-meat/

Jewell, T. (2023, March 30). *9 best hydration apps for 2023.* Healthline. https://www.healthline.com/health/hydration-top-iphone-android-apps-drinking-water

Jibrin, J. (2023, August 8). *Best anti-inflammatory foods—plus what to avoid.* Forbes Health. https://www.forbes.com/health/body/best-anti-inflammatory-foods/

Julia. (2023, August 5). *Dairy-free creamed spinach (keto, paleo, vegan).* The Roasted Root. https://www.theroastedroot.net/dairy-free-creamed-spinach-keto-paleo-vegan/

Karadsheh, S. (2022, September 7). *Easy turmeric chicken.* The Mediterranean Dish. https://www.themediterraneandish.com/mediterranean-roast-chicken-recipe-turmeric-fennel/

Karadsheh, S. (2023, June 6). *Easy ratatouille (one pot vegetable stew).* The Mediterranean Dish. https://www.themediterraneandish.com/easy-ratatouille-recipe/

Kenđel Jovanović, G., Mrakovcic-Sutic, I., Pavičić Žeželj, S., Šuša, B., Rahelić, D., & Klobučar Majanović, S. (2020). The efficacy of an energy-restricted anti-inflammatory diet for the management of obesity in younger adults. *Nutrients, 12*(11). https://doi.org/10.3390/nu12113583

Keyweo. (2021, August 3). *The importance of tracking weight loss progress.* https://www.spatzmedical.com/the-importance-of-tracking-weight-loss-progress/

Khan, S. (2022, May 2). *Shahi tukda to seviyan: The best Eid-ul-Fitr recipes that are healthy too!* Healthshots. https://www.healthshots.com/healthy-eating/recipes/healthy-eid-recipes-to-make-your-eid-ul-fitr-sweeter/

Killeen, B. L. (2020, June 19). *Raspberry-peach-mango smoothie bowl.* EatingWell. https://www.eatingwell.com/recipe/254618/raspberry-peach-mango-smoothie-bowl/

Killeen, B. L. (2021, October 26). *Mozzarella, basil & zucchini frittata.* EatingWell. https://www.eatingwell.com/recipe/251004/mozzarella-basil-zucchini-frittata/

Killeen, B. L. (20223, September 19). *Spinach-avocado smoothie.* EatingWell. https://www.eatingwell.com/recipe/262759/spinach-avocado-smoothie/

Killeen, B. L. (2023a, September 14). *Berry-kefir smoothie.* EatingWell. https://www.eatingwell.com/recipe/257793/berry-kefir-smoothie/

Killeen, B. L. (2023b, September 19). *Chickpea pasta with mushrooms & kale.* EatingWell. https://www.eatingwell.com/recipe/7939117/chickpea-pasta-with-mushrooms-kale/

Killeen, B. L. (2023c, September 19). *Honey-Mustard pork with spinach & smashed white beans.* EatingWell. https://www.eatingwell.com/recipe/260932/honey-mustard-pork-with-spinach-smashed-white-beans/

Kiser, T. (2022, December 15). *Healthy banana muffins with turmeric.* Food Faith Fitness. https://www.foodfaithfitness.com/now-muffins/

Klees, L. P. (n.d.). 2.2 – *Why is nutrition important to health? in Nutritional applications for a healthy lifestyle.* Penn State. https://psu.pb.unizin.org/nutr100/chapter/why-is-nutrition-important-to-health/

Lachtrupp, E. (2023, September 5). *7-day anti-inflammatory diet meal plan: 1,200 calories.* EatingWell. https://www.eatingwell.com/article/291500/7-day-anti-inflammatory-diet-meal-plan-1200-calories/

Lawler, M. (2023, February 24). *What is the anti-inflammatory diet? A detailed beginner's guide.* Everyday Health. https://www.everydayhealth.com/diet-nutrition/diet/anti-inflammatory-diet-benefits-food-list-tips/

Leech, J. (2019, June 11). *11 evidence-based health benefits of eating fish.* Healthline. https://www.healthline.com/nutrition/11-health-benefits-of-fish

Li, J., Lee, D. H., Hu, J., Tabung, F. K., Li, Y., Bhupathiraju, S. N., Rimm, E. B., Rexrode, K. M., Manson, J. E., Willett, W. C., Giovannucci, E. L., & Hu, F. B. (2020). Dietary inflammatory potential and risk of cardiovascular disease among men and women in the U.S. *Journal of the American College of Cardiology, 76*(19), 2181–2193. https://doi.org/10.1016/j.jacc.2020.09.535

Lichty, M. (2020, March 5). *Hearty vegetarian chili*. Two Peas & Their Pod. https://www.twopeasandtheirpod.com/hearty-vegetarian-chili/

Lifesum. (2022, March 15). *Five reasons to track your progress*. https://lifesum.com/nutrition-explained/five-reasons-to-track-your-progress

Lolley, P. (2023, September 19). *Blackberry smoothie*. EatingWell. https://www.eatingwell.com/recipe/7899650/blackberry-smoothie/

Lopez, W. (2023a, September 18). *Mixed-berry breakfast smoothie*. EatingWell. https://www.eatingwell.com/recipe/7959466/mixed-berry-breakfast-smoothie/

Lopez, W. (2023b, September 20). *Make-ahead freezer breakfast burritos with eggs, cheese & spinach*. EatingWell. https://www.eatingwell.com/recipe/7992201/make-ahead-freezer-breakfast-burritos-with-eggs-cheese-spinach/

Malcoun, C. (2019, September 6). *Greek salad with edamame*. EatingWell. https://www.eatingwell.com/recipe/257315/greek-salad-with-edamame/

Mandl, E. (2023, July 4). *12 great ways to get rid of bloating*. Healthline. https://www.healthline.com/nutrition/proven-ways-to-reduce-bloating

Mathis, A. (2023, September 18). *Lemon-berry ricotta toast*. EatingWell. https://www.eatingwell.com/recipe/8045884/lemon-berry-ricotta-toast/

McManus, K. D. (2019, January 31). *Why keep a food diary?* Harvard Health Publishing. https://www.health.harvard.edu/blog/why-keep-a-food-diary-2019013115855

Menza, K. (2017, August 28). *I lost 20 lbs on the anti-inflammatory diet — and fixed my skin forever*. Delish. https://www.delish.com/food/a55110/anti-inflammatory-diet/

Mervosh, L. (2023, September 19). *Vegan chickpea omelet*. EatingWell. https://www.eatingwell.com/recipe/7919697/vegan-chickpea-omelet/

Miller, S. (2023, February 9). *How to make chicken stock*. The Mediterranean Dish. https://www.themediterraneandish.com/how-to-make-chicken-stock

Mobin, A. (2023, March 23). *Anti-inflammatory diet: The key to menopause joint pain relief*. Cannabotech. https://cannabotech.com/a/s/answers/pain/anti-inflammatory-diet-the-key-to-menopause-joint-pain-relief

Morillo, E. (2023, June 14). *82 breakfast quotes to help you start your day (BEST)*. Gracious Quotes. https://graciousquotes.com/breakfast/

Narayana Health Blogs. (2023, January 25). *How to maintain a balanced diet*. https://www.narayanahealth.org/blog/how-to-maintain-a-balanced-diet/

National Heart, Lung, and Blood Institute. (2020, December 23). *Anti-inflammatory diets may reduce the risk of cardiovascular disease*. National Institutes of Health. https://www.nhlbi.nih.gov/news/2020/anti-inflammatory-diets-may-reduce-risk-cardiovascular-disease

National Library of Medicine. (2018, February 22). *What is an inflammation?* National Institutes of Health. https://www.ncbi.nlm.nih.gov/books/NBK279298/

NDTV Food Desk. (2017, October 6). *Health note: 6 important points to remember while buying meat*. NDTV. https://www.ndtv.com/food/6-important-points-to-remember-while-buying-meat-1759412

Newgent, J. (2023, September 19). *Breakfast salad with egg & salsa verde vinaigrette*. EatingWell. https://www.eatingwell.com/recipe/281188/breakfast-salad-with-egg-salsa-verde-vinaigrette/

Nicole. (2021, August 2). *Roasted green beans and mushrooms with walnuts*. Oh My Veggies. https://ohmyveggies.com/roasted-green-beans-and-mushrooms-with-walnuts/

Office H2O. (2020, March 11). *Tips to keep track of water intake*. https://www.officeh2o.com/2020/03/11/tips-to-keep-track-of-water-intake/

Pahwa, R., Goyal, A., & Jialal, I. (2023, August 7). *Chronic inflammation*. National Library of Medicine. https://www.ncbi.nlm.nih.gov/books/NBK493173/

Pain Doctor. (n.d.). *Citrus rosemary and sage rubbed turkey breast*. https://paindoctor.com/thanksgiving-recipe-citrus-rosemary-sage-rubbed-turkey-breast/

Pal, A. (2023, September 15). *Black salt: Uses, benefits, side effects, precautions & more!* PharmEasy Blog. https://pharmeasy.in/blog/ayurveda-uses-benefits-side-effects-precautions-of-black-salt/

Parle, A. (n.d.). *How to make a meal plan*. Safefood. https://www.safefood.net/how-to/meal-plan

Parsons, L. (2022, September 6). *13 sneaky inflammatory foods to remove from your kitchen*. FitOn. https://fitonapp.com/nutrition/inflammatory-foods/

Piedmont. (n.d.). *Anti-inflammatory diet*. https://www.piedmont.org/living-better/the-anti-inflammatory-diet

Raman, R. (2023, September 27). *How to do an elimination diet and why*. Healthline. https://www.healthline.com/nutrition/elimination-diet

Ramirez, B. (n.d.). *Pain scale chart*. Care Patron. https://www.carepatron.com/templates/pain-scale-chart

Rankin, K. (2023, May 20). *Easy stuffed mushrooms*. EatingWell. https://www.eatingwell.com/recipe/275734/easy-stuffed-mushrooms/

Robinson, K., & Zaremba, K. (2022, September 12). *The top anti-inflammatory foods list: 13 foods that fight inflammation*. Fullscript. https://fullscript.com/blog/anti-inflammatory-foods

Roth, S. (2020, November 2). *Avoiding inflammatory foods can lower heart disease, stroke risk*. American College of Cardiology. https://www.acc.org/about-acc/press-releases/2020/11/02/19/00/avoiding-inflammatory-foods-can-lower-heart-disease-stroke-risk

Sadasuvin, S., Oliver, L., Rao, G., Milch, H., Decker, A., Lenders, C., Gorman, K., LaMorte, W. W., Harvey, N., Stanfield, L., & Supple, V. (n.d.). *Dietary self-assessment*. Sphweb. https://sphweb.bumc.bu.edu/otlt/MPH-Modules/PH/NutritionModules/Dietary_Self_Assessment/Dietary_Self_Assessment_print.html

Save the Food. (n.d.). *10 easy tips for meal planning*. https://savethefood.com/articles/10-easy-tips-for-meal-planning

Seattle Sutton's Healthy Eating. (n.d.). *Reflecting on your weight loss journey*. https://www.seattlesutton.com/blog/reflecting-on-your-weight-loss-journey/

Seeds of Hope. (2020, January 22). *Busting the myths around teen nutrition*. https://www.seedsofhopesupport.com/teen-diet-and-nutrition-myths/

Snyder, C. (2023, April 19). *11 simple ways to adopt a healthy, sustainable eating pattern*. Healthline. https://www.healthline.com/nutrition/14-ways-to-stick-to-a-diet#3.-Lean-on-professionals-to-get-started

Spritzler, F. (2023, February 16). *Anti-Inflammatory diet 101: How to reduce inflammation naturally*. Healthline. https://www.healthline.com/nutrition/anti-inflammatory-diet-101

Taste of Home Editors. (2022, September 9). *Festive turkey meatballs*. Taste of Home. https://www.tasteofhome.com/recipes/festive-turkey-meatballs/

The Clean Eating Couple. (2022, October 15). *Green bean almondine recipe*. https://thecleaneatingcouple.com/healthy-green-beans-almondine/

The Clean Eating Couple. (2023, March 8). *Crispy roasted potatoes in oven*. https://thecleaneatingcouple.com/crispy-sheet-pan-roasted-potatoes/

TUFTS Health Plan. (n.d.). *The importance of good nutrition*. https://www.tuftsmedicarepreferred.org/healthy-living/importance-good-nutrition

University of Colorado Denver. (n.d.). *Dietary assessment methods [fact sheet]*. https://www.ucdenver.edu/docs/librariesprovider28/ctrc/nutrition/dietary-assessment-methods.pdf?sfvrsn=7e8865b9_2

USPM Care Team. (2021, April 7). *How to maintain a healthy eating lifestyle*. https://www.uspm.com/how-to-maintain-a-healthy-eating-lifestyle/

UW Integrative Health. (n.d.). *The elimination diet [fact sheet]*. https://www.fammed.wisc.edu/files/webfm-uploads/documents/outreach/im/handout_elimination_diet_patient.pdf

Valente, L. (2023a, September 19). *Peanut butter & jelly smoothie*. EatingWell. https://www.eatingwell.com/recipe/251039/peanut-butter-jelly-smoothie/

Valente, L. (2023b, September 19). *Peanut butter energy balls*. EatingWell. https://www.eatingwell.com/recipe/275207/peanut-butter-energy-balls/

Vespa, J. (2022, December 13). *Copycat Starbucks spinach & mushroom egg bites*. EatingWell. https://www.eatingwell.com/recipe/8018312/copycat-starbucks-spinach-mushroom-egg-bites/

Wang, J., Chen, W.-D., & Wang, Y.-D. (2020). The relationship between gut microbiota and inflammatory diseases: The role of macrophages. *Frontiers in Microbiology, 11*. https://doi.org/10.3389/fmicb.2020.01065

Wartenberg, L., & Spritzler, F. (2023, May 23). *Anti-Inflammatory foods to eat: A full list*. Healthline. https://www.healthline.com/nutrition/13-anti-inflammatory-foods

Waters, J. (2023, June 11). *The ultimate anti inflammatory diet for menopause*. Lyma Life. https://lyma.life/journal/menopause-diet-for-weight-loss/

WebMD Editorial Contributors. (2001, December 31). *Inflammation*. WebMD. https://www.webmd.com/arthritis/about-inflammation

Webster, K. (2023, September 19). *Spinach & feta scrambled egg pitas*. EatingWell. https://www.eatingwell.com/recipe/267878/spinach-feta-scrambled-egg-pitas/

Weniger, K. (2022, November 21). *Six anti-inflammatory recipes perfect for your holiday parties*. Institute for Integrative Nutrition. https://www.integrativenutrition.com/blog/antiinflammatory-holiday-recipes

Williams, M. (2023, September 19). *Lemon-blueberry yogurt toast*. EatingWell. https://www.eatingwell.com/recipe/7945123/lemon-blueberry-yogurt-toast/

Yoo, J. Y., Groer, M., Dutra, S. V. O., Sarkar, A., & McSkimming, D. I. (2020). Gut microbiota and immune system interactions. *Microorganisms, 8*(10), 1587. https://doi.org/10.3390/microorganisms8101587

Young, G. (2023, September 19). *Ginger beef stir-fry with peppers*. EatingWell. https://www.eatingwell.com/recipe/7885348/ginger-beef-stir-fry-with-peppers/

Zenbelly. (2019, August 21). *Apple sauce.* https://www.zenbelly.com/apple-sauce/

ZOE. (n.d.). *Gut health check: 5 signs of a healthy gut.* https://zoe.com/post/5-healthy-gut-signs